Both Sides of the Fire

FINIAL PUBLISHING

'This book is really a collection of short stories
about when I was on the railways in the days of steam
and then while serving as a Fire Officer in Nottingham,
before returning to the railways in preservation'.

DAVID L. THOMPSON

Both Sides of the Fire

First published 2006 by
FINIAL PUBLISHING

ISBN 1-900467-33-X

Produced by Finial Publishing
15 Abingdon Drive
Caversham Park
Reading
Berks
RG4 6SA
England

Tel/Fax: 0118-9484103

www.finial.co.uk
Email: mail@finial.co.uk

CONTENTS

INTRODUCTION

Starting work on the railways at Toton near Nottingham, first as an engine cleaner and then progressing to fireman, it began to look as if this would be my career forever.

Then, along with the change over from steam traction to diesel and the coming of Dr. Beeching, the future began to not look so good and with almost regular night work, especially as I had a young family, I decided to look elsewhere for employment.

I had joined the Nottinghamshire Fire Service as a retained fireman while still working on the railway and saw the Fire Service as a possible future career move.

Before this, I was informed of a job with the Fire & Safety Department of British Steel at Stanton and Stavely, near Ilkeston, Derbyshire.

This is where I went for a better future; unfortunately, shortly afterwards, I could see that this industry as well would soon be in decline, so taking a wage cut, I joined the Fire Service full time.

What I did not know was that steam still coursed through my veins and I would always love anything in steam.

Then, one day, I read an advertisement appealing for any ex-British Railways drivers and firemen to help to run the trains at the Midland Railway Centre at Butterley, Derbyshire, a heritage railway entirely run by volunteers.

After interview, medical and firing test, I was back on the footplate.

My first turn on returning was to be on Stanier Black 5 No. 44932, the event being covered by a reporter and cameraman from the Nottingham Evening Post, the idea being to use this event for publicity in an attempt to attract more volunteers to assist on this heritage railway.

The reporter had planned for about half-a-page of broadsheet, including the photograph and story and during my interview, he asked if I had ever thought of writing about my life on steam engines and on fire engines?

So, tongue in cheek, I said that I already had the title in mind and in his report in the newspaper, he wrote: "David is currently writing his autobiography" called 'Both Sides of the Fire'.

Although I had decided on a title, up at the time I had absolutely nothing on paper, so with people asking "Where was my book?", I decided to start writing - about pages!

This lay untouched for about 20 years.

So, retiring from the Fire Service after 31 years, I thought I would spend all my time working with steam preservation, but with divorce and later re-marriage, this was not to be and I found myself travelling the world in a completely new career, but that is another story in itself.

I still worked on steam whenever possible, sharing my work and experiences with Jean my new wife and it was Jean who encouraged me to put down some of my memories, especially so that our grandchildren could share them and have something to remember.

So, after 20 years, I started again and this is the result. I hope the final result is interesting and without too much detail.

Many thanks to all my ex-colleagues on the Railways and especially those in the Nottinghamshire Fire & Rescue Service where I loved every minute and more recently, all the people involved with steam preservation and heritage railways.

DAVID L. THOMPSON

David Leslie Thompson was born in the City of Nottingham in 1944, the middle son of three brothers who all worked on the footplate of steam locomotives at Toton. He then left the railway to work in the Fire department of Stanton Ironworks, near Ilkeston, Derbyshire, before joining Nottinghamshire Fire Service, serving first at West Bridgford. Leaving the fire service after 31 years service, he then started to work as a part time, self employed consultant.

Chapter one

Steam Driven into my Soul

Over the years, many books have been written about the work of steam locomotive footplate crews, so I was not really sure where to start, or how to make my recollections different from all the other books or stories. In the end, I thought to myself, just tell it as it was! After all, this is not really a book about railways, but more a set of stories about my life on and off the railway; during the time I spent working with steam on British Railways before leaving to join the Fire Service and returning to steam in the preservation era, enjoying the heritage railways and operating on the main line with preserved steam locomotives.

What were the reasons that made me want to start work on the railways? Was it in my blood? Had I dreamed of working on the railway? The answer to all of these is 'No!'. I had never thought of the railway in terms of a job, in fact I had never thought about the future and what I would do when the time came for leaving school.

As a child living in Trowell, named as the Festival of Britain village, the railways did have some connection with me, as 'train spotting' was part of the activities of the local kids. So was 'lorry spotting', collecting the numbers of the British Road Services lorries. However, the railway was always the more important to us.

Hours would be spent sitting on the grassy embankment overlooking Trowell Junction signal box. From here we would write down all the engine numbers, the highlight being the named engines that were often to be found at the head of the express trains using the Erewash Valley and Trowell branch lines. Train after train loaded with coal headed for Toton sidings and the south, with trains of empty wagons heading north, destined for all the many coalfields.

One day, and with the proceeds from my newspaper rounds, I was able to purchase my first 'Ian Allan ABC' of London Midland Region railway engines, where every LMR engine was listed.

However, as we all reached our teen years, some of us decided to travel to better 'spotting' locations and a Barton's bus ride from Trowell to Long Eaton, then a change to a Midland Red bus from Nottingham to Birmingham, would take us to Tamworth.

Here, armed with pens, my 'Ian Allan ABC', sandwiches and fizzy drink, we would spend the day at this Mecca for train spotters.

Other trips took us from Ilkeston North station to Grantham, via the magnificent Nottingham Victoria station. But, now an 'Ian Allan Combined Volume' was required, as only this book listed the locomotives of all the different regions; the Western, Southern and, of course, the North Eastern. At Grantham, we would see more named locomotives in one day than in over a month back in Trowell.

These giants of the East Coast Main Line were very special, especially Mallard the holder, even to this day, of the world speed record for a steam locomotive. Still looking powerful as it did all those years ago, today the locomotive has pride of place in the National Railway Museum at York.

Further trips were made to all the other regions to collect the numbers and discuss the merits of very different locomotives.

At this time, I never thought of a life on the railway and shortly afterwards I gave up train spotting, as I discovered something even more exciting!

I think it must have been something to do with my hormones, as one day, I found that I had more interest in the female form and shape than the models of Stanier and Gresley. So, the 'Ian Allan Combined Volume' was consigned to be put away, never to be used again.

The money I had previously spent on travelling all over the country had now been spent on a tailor-made suit with a silk lining and drainpipe trousers, winkle-picker shoes, a white shirt and a bootlace tie.

So, with Brylcreamed hair, complete with a quiff, it was off to the local dance hall, the Premier at Ilkeston. *(Sorry, I'm getting carried away and ahead of myself, as this happened after I left school and started work!)*

School for me then was Bramcote Hills Technical School at Bramcote Nottingham, where I went after passing my eleven plus examination. Some subjects bored me and neither of my parents pushed me, so I was content to just do enough to get by and 'bone idle' was the description used on some of my school reports. That is except for the hands-on subjects, such as woodwork, metalwork and technical drawing, subjects that I really enjoyed and did well in. French lessons? Who needed them, when the only travelling I had done was to the coast for the holidays and then I can only remember two holidays in my whole life.

I was very short-sighted about most things in the future during my school days, just taking each day as it happened. I had no ambitions and can only presume I was happy with life as it was.

Towards the end of my school life, I used to play a lot of truant along with other friends, something that I am not proud of, and in the process I lost out on my education. Realising that I would never pass my examinations in Maths, English, and Chemistry subjects, I decided that I would try to leave school at 15-years-of-age, instead of staying on at school until I was 16.

At this time, the education authority had very strict rules to prevent grammar school places being taken up, then being wasted by pupils leaving before completing their education. These rules stated that for each term missed, a charge would be levied; £50 if I remember, a lot of money at this time! Paying this fee would allow me to leave early and I remember borrowing the money from my eldest brother, as my parents did not have the means to pay. My intentions were to start work and pay him back.

All of my old mates from our village left secondary school at fifteen-years-of-age and started work, as obtaining employment was no problem in those days. My first job on leaving school had the grand title of trainee manager at an ironmonger's shop - Hall-Deacon in South Street, Ilkeston, Derby.

In reality, I was a general dogsbody who did all the work no one else wanted to do. I hated being stuck in a shop, where we were all ordered to call the customers 'Sir' or 'Madam' and I suppose I was a younger version of Granville played by David Jason in TV's 'Open all hours'.

The only exciting thing that happened to me at the shop was one day finding the married van driver kissing the young secretary at the back of the store yard, after which the driver threatened to 'put my lights out' if I ever told anyone. Well, even though it had taken over 40 years, maybe I should watch out!

But, there was no way could I come to terms with my life behind the counter of a shop, possibly for the next 50 years.

The only interesting parts of the job for me was helping out on the van delivering items to customers, but I did learn to cut all types of keys and also cut glass to size from the huge sheets delivered to us from the glassworks.

I also hated working Saturdays. Strange, but from then to the end of my working life, I have always worked Saturdays, Sundays and Bank holidays, in fact all the days the majority of people are on holiday.

My eldest brother worked on the railway as an engine cleaner and told me of the crowd of youths who worked and played together. This seemed far more exiting than the prospect of 50 years stuck in a shop, so boredom with my job was the real reason I looked towards working on the railways.

I started working on the railway in 1959, aged 15, as an engine cleaner at Toton Motive Power Depot (MPD), which lies in the centre of the then massive Toton marshalling yards, about midway between Nottingham and Derby on the Erewash Valley line.

This huge marshalling yard would deal with thousands of wagons every 24 hours. Destined for all parts of the country, the wagons conveyed every type of freight, but mainly coal.

Toton MPD provided the steam engines and crews to deal with these thousands of wagons that were formed up into trains, mainly coal to the south and west and the empty wagons on their way back to the Nottinghamshire, Leicestershire, Derbyshire and Yorkshire coalfields.

As far as I can recall, there had been no family history of railwaymen in our family, but within a short while, both my two brothers and myself were working at Toton in the footplate grades.

There was a slight problem with the starting of my railway career, because I did not reach the minimum height required for the job of engine cleaner, but I only found this out when I applied for the job. After having my height checked, they turned me down, being told to re-apply when I had grown a bit.

My eldest brother had already started straight from school and was a passed cleaner when I applied, so I was disappointed to be turned down in view of my height, or lack of it.

Luckily for me, shortly afterwards I met an old school pal who had just started work in the offices of British Railways at Toton and he told me one of his jobs was to measure applicants seeking work in the footplate grades. Pity he was not there the week before when I first applied! So, I applied again.

With a little stretching and some bending of the rules, via my old school mate,

I managed to be measured at the minimum height, with a medical at Derby to overcome before I started on the railway. Although I passed the medical, my height was questioned by the doctor, but finally he said while I looked under the minimum height, he was sure that Toton office had measured me correctly and the physical work would soon make me grow, so I was going to be a railwayman - or boy.

Unlike now, jobs were easy to come by at this time, so there was quite a turnover of staff. They quickly moved on when they found they did not like the work or the shift work, dirty conditions and especially the money which was not very good. I seem to recall that my starting wage was about £3-4s-0d per week or £3-20p in today's money. Less than I earned on my newspaper rounds as a school boy!

The bonus was that you were not on a production line, or confined indoors during your workday. There were other lads of more-or-less the same age as yourself working together and the prospects seemed good, with the final outcome of becoming an engine driver.

No one at Toton had even heard of Dr. Beeching at this time, or even thought about the rapid demise of steam locomotives, or the railways themselves that would shortly be about to happen.

Engine cleaning was the first rung on the ladder of the 'footplate grade' as it was then called and the railways were desperately short of young men, due to the low wages and better paid other work available in other industries.

Initially, when you started work, you were issued with two pairs of navy blue coloured cotton bib and brace overalls, jackets and a grease-top hat. You had to provide your own boots, although one thing I was never issued with was a cap badge. Despite numerous requests, the stores man never appeared to have any.

You were then given your number, which was stamped on a brass token; this is what you used to sign on and off duty and to draw materials from the stores. On Fridays, this token would be exchanged for another one, which you then handed to the wages clerk in exchange for your weekly wages. Wages were paid in cash in a little brown envelope, showing your deductions for tax and National Insurance in ink, having been filled in by hand on the front of the envelope.

On my first day, I had to report to the running foreman before being introduced to the charge-hand cleaner. I was then escorted around the engine sheds and surrounding areas by a more senior cleaner. Later, we were given the number or numbers of the engines that our team had to clean and after drawing cloths, brushes and two different cleaning fluids from the stores, we set to work.

Daily, the cleaners, including myself, would arrive at work in the morning and report to the charge-hand cleaner. He would allocate the engines to us after he had had a consultation with the Running Foreman as to which engines required cleaning. Looking back, they all required cleaning; even after our efforts they still looked filthy!

Before allocation of the cleaning tasks, the charge-hand foreman would hand out labouring jobs to the senior cleaners. At this time, the railways found it hard to recruit labourers, as the money was poor and the work, hard and dirty. Most of these jobs were filled by immigrants seeking a better life in the UK, but still many jobs remained unfilled.

These jobs included emptying the ash pits, many tons of ash and clinker being dropped into the pits every 24 hours by the large number of steam engines coming onto the sheds for service. The smokebox-end of the steam locomotive's boiler collected ash that was called 'char' and this had to be cleaned out of the smokebox. Eventually, it would be loaded into wagons for disposal. Char is very fine and so was easily blown about, so the labourers were very quickly covered, especially if they were sweating and the char would stick to your skin like glue, quickly changing your appearance from white to a shiny black. This is the ash that gets in your eyes and hair when looking out the carriage windows when a train is pulled by a steam engine.

To stop a locomotive's wheels slipping on the rails when under load, dry sand was used. This was another physical job. Firstly, 16-ton wagon loads of wet sand had to be shovelled into the sand house on the first floor (imagine unloading a 16-ton lorry load of wet sand into your bedroom, by hand with a shovel via the bedroom window and you have the picture of the job).

At least you were in a warm and dry place to do this, as the sand house was under cover. You were also told that you could go home as soon as the 16-tons had been emptied. If you worked too hard and finished the task too quickly, the charge-hand cleaner would renege on his promise, so you learned to finish about an hour before the end of your shift and then he let you go home early. The sand house contained three massive cast-iron stoves on the first floor, where the wet sand was dried. The sand when dried then flowed down to the ground floor.

These stoves had to be fired-up and the wet sand loaded around them, which with the amount used at Toton, was a full time job.

The sand house at Toton was looked after by a man called Henry Dicker, who worked regular nights. He was a large and rather strange man who frightened the life out of the cleaners. He was a real loner and very odd, but who when left alone was OK. However, cleaners being young men, they used to wind him up and he could become quite irrational. We would be warned off upsetting him, because although strange, he did his job well.

It was always rumoured that a wagon door accidentally opened smashing him on the head and knocking him to the ground, in the process breaking his leg in the fall and leaving him brain damaged. However, as far as we knew this was a rumour, but he did have mad eyes and his family were all eccentrics, to put it mildly.

Back to the labouring positions, many of which were vacant, but still needed doing, so the cleaners were given these jobs. On these occasions, the locomotives were not cleaned, as all the cleaners were labouring, but it would have been difficult to know this, as all the engines looked filthy unless they had just come from the works. Cleaning was just a token job to fill in, until you were old enough to be passed out to do a fireman's job.

The bonus for the cleaners doing the labourer's job was that you were paid the daily rate of a labourer. Their wage was £8-8s-0d a week, or £8-40p today, quite a wage rise, if you were lucky enough to labour all week. It was mainly in the day time when they were short of labour, because shift enhancement especially the night shifts made the jobs more profitable.

This labouring wage was the same as a fireman's pay, the next but one rank on the footplate grade.

The charge-hand cleaner was very busy, his words not mine, so he did not have too much time to chase up the cleaners and mainly would tour the engine sheds at the same time each day. It did not take much brain power to ensure that everyone would be cleaning when he arrived, unless we thought we had finished the job and did not want to start another one.

Toton had three sheds, called roundhouses because the engines were stabled around the turntables in each of the sheds, although they were in fact, square shaped buildings. Over 150 engines were based at Toton, all freight engines, with the exception of the engine kept to do all the shed shunting and this was also the cleanest engine, as it had a regular crew. No. 41947 was a passenger tank engine that had been originally based in the Tilbury area before being pensioned off to Toton, where I understand it was sent to work the short branch line from Ilkeston Junction to Ilkeston Town.

Occasionally, the odd passenger engine would find its way to Toton, but they were not suited to the loose coupled freight trains that dominated the Toton trains, so were not much use to the foreman who wanted heavy freight locomotives. Passenger engines were all right on fully fitted freight trains, but these were rare from Toton, although there were some semi-fitted trains.

One train that was always fully fitted was the 'Ghost Train'; this train originated at Shipley Colliery and was worked to Toton via the Stanton branch by a Class 4 Fowler 0-6-0 engine. The train was made up of special fitted 40-ton coal wagons and ran only at night from Toton to Willesden, hauled by a Class 8 Stanier 2-8-0. The empty wagons returned to Toton overnight, hence the name 'Ghost Train'.

The size and distances the charge-hand cleaner had to travel around the sheds made it easy for us young cleaners to avoid him and hide from him and as young men, we did this on a regular basis. When he was unable to find us, he would threaten all sorts of retribution, including the sack when we reported to him at the end of the shift. He had a difficult job because the railway was short of suitable men or youths, so they wanted to hang on to the ones they had. We were well aware of this and exploited it to the limit, but the charge-hand cleaner still had to answer to the foreman when a job had not been completed, so he had a rotten job, but we did not worry too much about his problems in those days.

In the canteen at Toton, some things were always certain; water would always be boiling to make a can of tea and there was always a card school in progress, as crews awaited the call from the foreman for their next job, or were on a meal break while working a shed turn. Sometimes playing for large sums of money, it did not take long before the cleaners knew all the card games in theory, but actually playing them was another thing. This knowledge did not come cheap, as you had to lose money to learn the skills required to 'brag' so as to win the kitty, brag being the game most played in the mess room. The other game played was cribbage, a game played by two people, so ideally suited to driver and fireman on the footplate. Most firemen carried a pack of cards and a cribbage board in his bag, along with his pack up, tea and milk.

I remember loosing a week's wages in one game, playing brag in the mess room, before deciding not to get involved with these card schools again.

To pass the shift along, the cleaners would climb inside the firebox of the engine and play cards for peanuts, much to the anger of the charge-hand, who could not find them, because he would not normally look into the firebox while searching for them. Another place was at the top of the coal-hopper, as no charge-hand ventured up there. So, we had lots of places to hide and we used them. We also ventured further afield. Next door was Corry's, an old wagon repair shed, which had loads of interesting parts to roam and hide.

This was on the site of the present Toton Diesel Maintenance Depot. Long Eaton was the nearest town and at weekends some cleaners even visited the cinemas while on duty. In fact, we got away with murder!

Life went on and then we had to work night shift cleaning and I have to admit there was more sleeping than cleaning done in those early years on night shift and no charge-hand cleaner. I don't remember doing many night shifts as a cleaner, but I did a few of them.

The next grade up from cleaning was a passed-cleaner, when you were passed out by an inspector to be allowed to perform the duties of a fireman, as and when required.

You were sent on a week's course prior to your examination. I was sent with some more cleaners to Westhouses shed, where we learned the basics in firing techniques, signalling and rules and regulations. Almost all the instructions were theoretical, with very little practical instruction.

You were expected to have picked up some practical experience while cleaning in the shed. This was done by helping crews in their preparation and disposal of their engines. The drivers and firemen would teach you how to build up a fire and how to work the injectors. The golden rule being, do not let the boiler water out of sight, thus causing the fusible plug to melt. This would result in the failure of the engine, possible damage to the firebox and you being disciplined by the shed foreman.

I was sent on the course to be a passed cleaner only a short time before my sixteenth birthday. You were not allowed to be passed out for the footplate until you were 16 years of age. An exception was made in my case, because it was only a short time until my sixteenth birthday and they were short of passed cleaners.

I'm not sure how many of us were sent on the course from Toton and I can't remember whether it was two or three.

We would sign on duty at Toton, then walk to Stapleford and Sandiacre station to catch the Sheffield train up the Erewash Valley to Westhouses & Blackwell station, a short walk again and we arrived at Westhouses shed, where our training would be held.

The classroom was a large wooden shed that had a bench seat running around a long wooden table. A blackboard and easel stood at one end.

Our instructor was a young passed fireman, who regularly attended the Mutual improvement courses at Toton.

We were instructed in the basics of correct firing techniques and the avoidance of making smoke, as even in 1959, you could be prosecuted for making excessive smoke.

Rules and regulations were on the agenda, special attention being paid to any that directly applied to the duties of a fireman. The rest you were expected to learn yourself by reading the books of rules and working practices that were issued to you.

Signalling was also covered; what were all the different signals and where they were placed and most importantly, what they indicated. How to protect a train in the event of any emergency by the use of detonators and red flags, or lamps. This was followed by a walk along the nearby lines, observing the signalling and track work.

When all the rules and regulations and all other matters had been covered, we finally came round to the steam engine.

What was steam? How was it produced and how was it harnessed and put to work?

What was coal? What did it consist of and how best to use it to ensure a plentiful supply of steam for the requirements of the driver?

How to manage the engine, to work it in the most economic way, avoiding the waste of coal and water by excessive blowing off. Keeping the footplate clean and tidy and observing all the signals when not actually firing.

The footplate was explained including all the parts and how and why they worked. The injectors, live steam operated and exhaust steam operated were drawn and explained. All of this was to be copied into our notebooks. The week went really fast, especially as you had to study at home ready for your examination the next week by the shed master at Toton.

The examination was an oral examination on all the points covered during the previous week.

I was successful in the examination and told that when I was 16 years old, which was not very far off, I would be qualified to act as a passed cleaner, carrying out the duties of a fireman when required. I was also issued with my handbook for Railway Steam Locomotive Enginemen. I still have the book, which is dated 11-11-60 and which has my name on the fly leaf of the book, which had been added by the shed master at the time.

However, I would be expected to keep up with my studies all the time that I would be on the footplate, so that eventually you could become a driver.

All that would be a long way off, as the average age that a fireman at Toton became a driver was the mid-forties. So, any fireman at Toton could look forward to nearly 30 years on the shovel.

No wonder many men transferred to other depots where promotion to driver could happen in their late twenties or early thirties, especially areas like London, or Birmingham where lots of other better paid jobs were available, so leaving the railways without sufficient manpower.

Many firemen from Toton went on loan to other depots, especially in the London and Birmingham areas.

On loan, there was always plenty of overtime, worked on your rest days and especially on Sundays so boosting their wages. The chance of promotion to passed firemen, or even to driver happened much quicker than at Toton. Many in their late twenties were passed for driving. Some men made these loans permanent by transfer to these depots.

When these loan periods finished and they moved back to Toton, they had to revert back to their previous jobs. So, even if they had been passed for driving, they were put back to firing at Toton, until their seniority allowed them to drive. With this setback, plus the reduction in pay, many of them made a permanent move, or left the railways for other better paid jobs.

Later on when I became a registered fireman, my application to go on loan to Saltley depot in Birmingham was refused as Toton was short of fireman, because many of the Toton firemen on loan never came back.

Chapter Two

Passed Cleaner

My first footplate duty was on my sixteenth birthday, the 2nd December 1960. The day before, the 'caller-up' had brought a slip of paper to my house to tell me of my change of duty. I was to sign on duty at 21.45 hrs for fireman's duty on a shunting turn in Toton north sidings. Not the hardest of jobs, but you had to start somewhere. So, this was to be the start of my footplate career proper.

Most skills needed to operate a steam locomotive were learned while in the shed as a cleaner, but it was very different from being in charge of the fire and boiler on your own, outside the confines of the shed. It was also different being on an engine in the dark, when everything seemed different; especially the shunter's light signals, or whistle signals. If you had to make a shunt over the humps at Toton, you were controlled by a series of white electric shunting signals.

When not required for footplate duties, you were back in the shed, labouring, or even still cleaning, but as time went on, more time was spent firing.

Going back to the 'caller up', the man who delivered the note to inform me on my birthday about my first firing turn. Before my time on the railway, the job of 'caller up' was one that the cleaners would perform. They would go and wake up drivers and firemen at all hours of the night, so that they reported for duty on time and did not oversleep.

If the duty that a driver, fireman, or passed cleaner changed from that rostered, the 'caller up' would have to get on his push bike and deliver the notification to their homes. Not a problem, as many drivers and firemen lived close to the engine sheds, however, they were not too keen calling up to my home, because I lived five miles away, a 10-mile round trip. They went ballistic when my two brothers and I were all called up during the same shift, but at different times, three round trips totalling 30-miles; they were seeing my mother more than my dad was!

Most turns firing were on the local shunting engines, or on the preparation of locomotives, ready for the crews to take straight off the shed for their day's work, the engines being coaled, oiled and having the fire prepared.

The opposite was the disposal of locomotives coming onto the shed, where they would normally be stabled near the coal hopper.

A crew of driver and fireman would then be allocated the first engine in line for disposal. Filling the tender with coal from the coal hopper would be the first job, then placing the locomotive over the ash pits to clean out the dirty fire and clinker from inside the firebox, finally raking out the ash from the ash pan underneath. If the engine was being used again, a small amount of clean fire would be left in the firebox. If the engine was due to have the boiler washed out, or be in for any repairs, then all the fire would be cleaned out.

Different methods were used depending on the type of fire bars fitted. The majority of engines at Toton had fixed fire bars. Using a bar fitted with a type of hook, about four fire bars would be pulled up and left in the firebox. The clinker and ash would then be pushed though the gap into the ash pan. Sometimes, broken bars, or bars, which had accidentally dropped into the ash pan had to be removed from underneath the engine in the ash pit, from where the ash pan would be raked clean. This was a dirty hot job, as standing on the red hot ash left cleaned from previous engines, you were breathing in the dust and sulphurous fumes produced in the confines of the ash pit. The more modern, mainly standard design engines had a rocking grate. On these types the theory was that you rocked the grate open and the clinker and ash fell through into the hopper ash pan. If heavily clinkered, the clinker would jam the rocking grate and cause even more work, but in the main, fire disposal in them was a lot easier.

This dirty job was followed by opening the smokebox door and emptying out the ash (or char), an equally dirty job that created lots of very fine dust that readily stuck to your already sweaty face. The driver would be examining the locomotive for any visible defects, any repair cards also having to be in by the driver. Water would be taken now, before the engine was stabled where the foreman required it and this could be inside or outside the shed.

By this time, on occasions, the steam pressure could be very low and it was a delicate job to take the engine into the shed, turn it via the turntable and then reverse it into its bay in the roundhouse. The turntables at Toton were operated by a vacuum motor, via the engine vacuum brake pipe.

However, if the steam pressure was too low, the engine would not be able to create a vacuum and so the turntable had to be turned manually by way of a cranked handle. Hard work, especially if the engine was not balanced perfectly on the turntable.

The walls around the shed bore the scars where, perhaps because of low steam pressure, the brakes were less efficient, or perhaps also lack of experience, the locomotive's buffers ended up going through the walls, resulting in reports and possible suspensions for driver, fireman or both.

The system in operation was that each locomotive was allocated a time for its disposal. When a crew had disposed of engines equal to their shifts, they were able to go home early. This resulted in crews racing each other to dispose of their engines and be ready for the next one. Sometimes, the fireman, or passed cleaner, would take the engine into the shed on their own, very much against the rules, while the driver went back for the next one, very often getting the cleaners to give them a hand.

There were always engines waiting for disposal in the early 1960s. The crews on these disposal turns were very often young drivers, or passed firemen and even younger firemen, so most were very fit and it was quite common to go home early. The full shifts work could be done in three hours, or less if you really worked hard without any breaks, plus you cut as many corners as possible.

For instance, if when you opened the smokebox door, no char fell out, then you would close up the smokebox door. Not like today, when they are really cleaned out.

Sometimes, if the engine had a 'SC' plate on the front, indicating that self-cleaning apparatus was fitted, we never even opened the door.

We only did all of this when we knew the engine was going to go 'off shed' again, so our negligence would not be discovered.

If the engine was going to be 'stopped' in the shed, then we had to clean out the smokebox, because if a fitter or boilersmith had to work inside the smokebox and reported that it had not been properly cleaned, we, the disposal crew would have been in trouble.

The same could be applied to cleaning out the ash pans, all of which gained us some time, so finishing our shift early.

At Toton, we had a disposal crew reporting for work every hour and at some peak times, two crews reporting together. Not all the crews wanted to go home early, so some were eager to let you have the work, but they were still paid if they did not dispose of their quota.

A smart move was to have a look at the condition of the fire in the next engine for disposal. If it had a huge fire and was badly clinkered up, you did not report that you were ready until you saw that the engine was allocated to another crew. Then you took the next engine, ensuring that you used another ash pit, or you would be stuck behind the engine with the bad fire that would take longer to dispose of. So, your engine was in the shed first and you were ready for the next one.

The crews preparing engines going off the shed, worked to the same rules, but the work to prepare engines was more time consuming, so you could never finish as early as the disposing crews.

The problems associated with preparing were if the engine had little or no fire, which meant that you had to raise the steam pressure enough to move the locomotive from the shed out into the sidings.

As steam diminished, so did a lot of these turns and waiting around in the mess room was the norm.

The canteen was the place where the world was put right; where the merits of men and locomotives were discussed and, of course, where the card schools were. During one of these informal talks, the merits of the steam brakes fitted to a Standard 9F was the subject. One side was for the brakes, the other side convinced that they were rubbish, especially when down on steam pressure. After much discussion, it was decided to put the brakes to the test.

Led by the driver who was adamant that the brakes were good, a plan was hatched to prove, or not, the efficiency of the brakes. He was prepared to hang his watch on the buffers of another engine, bring the 9F close to this engine and only using the steam brake, stop as close as he dare.

Waiting until a 9F was ready to enter the shed from off the ash pits, the party gathered eagerly to witness this scientific test.

Gently opening the regulator, the engine moved slowly towards the other engine, until very slowly the buffers met.

"Has it stopped?", the driver of the 9F asked.

"No! But your bloody watch has!"

Other regular jobs were the Toton stowers. These three jobs operated throughout 24-hours. They were one up on the shunting turns, as they moved trains between the various sidings at Toton and the surrounding area. The motive power was either a Fowler 4F 0-6-0, or a Stanier 8F 2-8-0. These were on stand by with engine and guard, to await whatever work came their way.

They were used to take trains to Chaddesden yard at Derby, or the yards at Beeston, Stanton Gate, Codnor Park, or Nottingham and were very often dependant on the route knowledge of the driver or guard.

These turns were worked by drivers on the 'old men's link', who did not want to work far from their base. They could be very boring one day and very different the next.

Servicing of the locomotives would take place on Toton shed when required and usually taken during a period when waiting for work.

One turn that could be allocated to the stowers was to take the Toton breakdown train to a mishap or crash.

When the breakdown train was called for, any engine, or crew could be called on to take out this train and this was the only turn at Toton where the express headlight code was carried.

If it was fairly local and on the route card of the driver, the Stanier 8F on the stower would be used.

The train would consist of three coaches and the Toton 75-ton steam crane, which was brought to steam pressure very quickly by one of the breakdown gang.

This gang was made up of mainly fitters who were on call 24-hours every day. They would respond immediately if on duty, but others would be called out from their homes.

The Toton breakdown train also carried a large set of hydraulic water jacks. With many wooden packing blocks and steel rollers, these jacks would soon have the majority of derailments back onto the rails, not forgetting the skills of the breakdown gang in operating the equipment.

One of the most crucial men was the cook; he had a kitchen permanently stocked with both fresh and canned food so as to sustain the gang over sometimes long and arduous shifts.

This gang could be called anywhere in the country if a large crash should occur, so they never knew how long they would be away. Thankfully large incidents were very rare.

The breakdown train was very important, so that after leaving Toton it would run as an express and have priority over any other trains. This also applied to the other breakdown trains around the various regions of the railway when going to any mishap.

Sometimes, non-urgent calls were made on this train, for example, when wagons had become derailed, but had not blocked any lines and so there was no urgency. In these circumstances, the breakdown train would be called out in the daytime and proceed at normal speed.

Some days, some unusual jobs would come out of the blue - like the breakdown train. Signing on for duty one day as a sixteen-year-old passed cleaner, my driver for the day was a passed fireman. After signing on duty, we were sent to the canteen to await instructions, as we were a spare crew brought on duty to cover any turn that was required. Sometimes on these turns, you could sit the entire shift without being called upon. On other days, you walked alongside the line to relieve crews on trains, waiting to enter Toton sidings who had completed their shift.

This day, after about an hour on duty, the driver was called to the foreman's office for instructions on a job. "Get your bag", he said returning to the mess room, "We have a job".

"Have you been on the main line, yet?", he asked as we walked to Toton Centre signal box, where there was an enginemen's cabin and where we were to wait to relieve the crew of a train.

"Why? Where are we going?", I asked.

" Masboro", he replied, "A London-Leeds fitted freight is running very late and the crew wants relief".

Masboro? I had no idea where it was, but I did know it was as far north as Toton crews went at that time, so it must be a long way off.

The train eventually arriving with a Stanier 8F at the front, deputising for a failed Stanier Black 5, we quickly climbed aboard. I had never seen a fire like the one in the firebox, the fire halfway up the fire hole and the coal in the tender well back. "Keep the fire well up", said the old fireman who I relieved "And you will be OK".

No sooner were we aboard, than the crew we relieved climbed off, the guard gave us the right away and we set off on the main line, up the Erewash valley.

This was an unusual turn for Toton men, as most of the work was with loose-coupled trains and my driver was determined to show how to work a fast freight. We stormed away from Toton Centre with full regulator and 55% cut-off. The noise was such that crews on the shed were all looking to see what was happening, as Toton men were normally very sedate with their loose-coupled trains.

As we stormed up the Erewash Valley, I never had much chance to look out as I was continually firing, or pulling forward coal in the tender. Eventually, the driver tapped me on the shoulder, "Well done lad, you've nearly done. All down hill from here".

We stopped to take water in the platform at Chesterfield station and then we were off again.

With the safety valves lifting, we came to a stand at Masboro, where we were relieved.

Walking into the enginemen's cabin on the station platform, we looked forward to filling our tea can and eat our pack up. But, the phone was ringing as we walked into the cabin and my driver, who picked up the receiver, was told, "Toton crew; your train is waiting to be relieved in the loop".

We then walked to the sidings to relieve a crew on an Austerity 8F with a loose-coupled train bound for Toton. Before we even had the chance to sit down, we were given the road and we were off.

We had a clear run all the way to Toton, which was very rare occurrence. It was also my first experience firing with a tender full of small goose egg-sized 'ovoids', which were made from coal dust compressed in some sort of mould. Because of their shape, the ovoids could quickly be all over the footplate and if the fire was not kept bright, would form dense clinker, which had to be cleaned out. The crews had a special name for them, which I could never repeat in this politically correct time. Arriving at Toton sidings, we unhooked from the train and took the engine on to the engine shed for disposal.

This being my first main line turn, this experience left me both physically tired, but also thrilled to bits that I had been up to it. Even in those days, some older drivers would not take young inexperienced firemen out on the main line, but word of my exploits soon got around and I was never refused.

The more experienced you became, resulted in you personally becoming more physically fit, which meant that you even got to look at the scenery on occasions and so the job did not seem so physical. The trip to Masboro was really only a short return journey, but at the time it seemed to me to be like it was a long trip.

Normally, only slow loose-coupled trains would leave Toton for the north. The journey would mostly be slow and involve many stops before being relieved at Masboro. Toton men always got relieved at Masboro, so did not sign for the road beyond there at this time, although this changed when through working to York came along. Working a train back to Toton as well, would often involve overtime working, so my baptism was all the more remarkable, especially since we had done it well inside our 8-hour shift, despite some time sitting in the mess room at Toton before we were given the job.

Another early memory I had was of one Saturday, again with a passed fireman. Signing on for duty, I was told by the foreman that I was to work the Toton-Northampton and given the name of my driver for the day. It was a name I had not heard before, but was told he was a young passed fireman. 'Young' was a term used to describe any passed fireman and nothing to do with his age, especially at Toton where it was quite the normal for firemen to be in their forties before being passed to drive.

I made my way to the wooden shed, where a large board was fastened to the walls. This was where engines were allocated to all the jobs leaving Toton. It was a huge board, covering all the turns worked over each 24-hours.

It would list the turn e.g. 10.00 Toton-Northampton and the engine number, usually a Stanier Class 8, or a Standard Class 9. Sometimes, the job was cancelled for different reasons; no traffic, no guard available, or even no engine available. In these cases the word 'Caped' was written in the place of the engine number.

This day I was surprised to see we were rostered a LNER engine, a Thompson B1 4-6-0 Class 5 mixed traffic engine.

This turn on a Saturday was worked to Market Harborough, where we were relieved by a crew from either Market Harborough, or Northampton. We then travelled as passengers to Leicester to work a train back to Toton.

Making my way to the engine that had been prepared by another crew, I came across this filthy engine and climbing aboard, I met my driver.

"Have you ever worked one of these engines?", he asked.

"No, I have never even been on one, ever!"

"Well, it will be a first for us both then!", he said.

Taking in the footplate, it was a clutter of pipes and valves and the fire hole had a big door hinged on one side. In the middle of the door was a flap through which you shovelled the coal. Fine with small pieces of coal, but at Toton some lumps could be about 2-cwt in size, so lots of extra work for the fireman breaking up the lumps to fit the flap. Sometimes, you would have the opposite and the tender would be filled with slack, or very fine coal almost dust, which made firing hard work as the coal tended to go straight out of the chimney if the engine was worked hard. So, you had to continually fire large amounts, the result being a dirty fire that had to be cleaned regularly.

Today that is what we had. Easy to shovel through the flap, but hard to maintain both steam pressure and keep a clean fire.

With no instructions, it was a matter of trial and error to operate the essential controls and we were off to the sidings for our train.

The line from Market Harborough to Northampton was very steeply graded and also went through single line tunnels that never emptied of smoke. Because of the steep grade, loading was restricted. Today, we had only a Class 5 locomotive, so only had a fairly light loose-coupled train. Leaving Toton, we passed Trent station and were surprised to be turned out onto the main line towards Loughborough and Leicester.

My driver then started to enjoy himself, as we made a fast run along the main line, whistling and waving to the other Toton crews as we passed the other numerous freight trains heading south on the slow line.

We were obviously making good time, as we were kept main line through Leicester and on towards Market Harborough. I was kept busy on the shovel due to my enthusiastic driver and the poor quality coal in the tender, most of which appeared to be 6-tons of dust and not the normal large lumps. Keeping a decent wedge-shaped fire was almost impossible, but the engine steamed well despite this and at least, I did not have to break up the normal large lumps of coal to get it through the flap.

The driver said to me he was glad we were to be relieved, because as you had to fire continually, the climb to Northampton would be a real test with this coal,. The climb to Northampton was through single line tunnels that were continually full of smoke and steam, making breathing very difficult, even when not firing. The idea was to build up a large fire before the tunnels, then you could get on the floor to try and get some air. Very difficult with this coal, as large amounts of slack would black out the fire and clinker up very quickly.

Eventually, we were running down the gradient towards Market Harborough and I was able to sit down and look out. I had never been at this speed on a coal train and it was then I noticed the look of alarm on the driver's face. He informed me that the brakes were not holding and we were running away! Whistling furiously as we approached Market Harborough to warn the signalman, he had the engine in reverse gear as we went through the station platform, past our relief crew and past the water crane. Luckily we had the signals thanks to the signalman.

Finally coming to a stop a few lengths past the water column, we contacted the signalman to obtain permission to set back to the water column. Then we were relieved and walked back to the station to catch the train to Leicester. Having some time spare, the driver took me to the nearby hotel where he bought me a pint of beer. I was still only sixteen and remember the barmaid commenting that I did not look old enough to be drinking. The driver told her you were not allowed on the main line less than 18-years-of-age, which satisfied her.

We then caught our train to Leicester to finish the rest of our turn without any other problems.

I was firing every day now and soon it was confirmed that I was to be made a registered fireman. This meant that I would be placed on a link rostered with a regular driver. Most of the turns worked on this link were trips to the many coal mines in the Nottinghamshire and Derbyshire areas, where coal was brought into Toton sidings, or to the many coal fired power stations in the Trent Valley

Many of the turns at Toton were to the various coal mines to take in empty wagons and bring out the loaded coal, destined eventually for all points of the country.

One important aspect of firing was to have a good set of tools, shovel, coal pick, bucket and spanners. Towards the end of steam, it was sometimes difficult to find these, so shovels were hidden for your own use. The coal pick was especially important at a freight depot. The coal supplied could range from almost dust to the biggest lumps, perhaps being three-foot long and two-foot wide. These had to be broken into fist-sized pieces and only a skilled fireman with a good coal pick could do this. Hard work when you had a tender full of big lumps, because as soon as you broke them up, they had to be shovelled into the firebox, then start on the next lump, double the work of evenly sized coal used at passenger engine sheds.

It was not unknown for the fireman to loose his grip on the shovel, especially when very tired, with the result that the shovel was lost into the firebox and even if recovered, the handle would be burnt away in seconds.

This never happened to me, but one day I was firing a Standard 9F on a Toton to Washwood Heath. Leaving Trent station it was a steep climb from a standing start to Sheet Stores Junction. As I pushed the shovel into the tender, a large lump wedged itself in the opening. In trying to move it with the shovel, I broke the shaft. So, I had no option but to fire the 9F with just the blade of the shovel until we reached Burton-upon-Trent. Here we stopped and I went into the engine shed to obtain a replacement.

We knew that if we carried on to Washwood Heath and then went on to Saltley engine shed, the odds were that you might not be able to find a spare shovel.

On Sundays, up to six crews of drivers and firemen were sent by a 12-seat bus from Toton to Saltley depot at Birmingham to bring back engines that belonged to Toton.

These engines had finished their turns, finally ending up at Saltley, but they needed to be sent back. At this time, Saltley was short of engine men, so they did not have the crews to do this.

Preparing your engine at Saltley was always a problem, as the tools needed were in short supply, i.e. shovel, coal pick, lamps and especially gauge glass lamps, bucket and spanners.

Sometimes you had to wait for an engine to come onto the shed so as to get the required kit and with six crews all searching, you had to be quick.

This was during the rundown of steam, when more diesels were appearing. In theory, there should have been plenty of tools, but certainly not so in reality.

A mystery really and I have wondered if the store men had huge stocks of new tools that they did not want to issue, because when steam finally finished at Toton, I remember wagons full of tools, lamps and oil containers etc being sent for scrap. Unfortunately, I did not save any of these which today would be collector's items.

Chapter Three

Swanwick and Other Stories

One day I was on the trip to Swanwick colliery, which is where nowadays the Midland Railway Centre is located. This turn was worked by a Fowler 0-6-0 4F tender locomotive, the empty wagons having to be backed inside the sidings and propelled up the single line to the colliery sidings. Because the line was very steeply inclined, only a few wagons at a time could be propelled up the incline, the engine being worked flat out with full regulator and 75% cut off. Sometimes, due to the conditions, we would stall on the incline and have to go back down for another push.

If the engine was not in good condition, of which many were not, the engine would prime and again we would stall on the incline (priming is when water is carried into the regulator valve and the cylinders, which can result in serious damage).

Bringing out the coal involved stopping to pin down the brakes on the wagons and very cautiously coming down the bank and stopping near to Swanwick signalbox. This particular morning, we arrived on the main line and were held at the signals. The fireman was required to proceed to the signalbox under Rule 55 and sign the book, making sure the signalman was aware of your train.

As I went to the desk to sign the book, I accidentally knocked the signalman's fountain pen off, which ended up with the nib stuck into the linoleum-covered floor.

"My new pen, you clumsy sod", he cried, or something like that!

Well, the pen nib was knackered, a pure accident, but the signalman was very angry and I was banished from his box. Little did I know then that this was where I would be reintroduced to the footplate many years later.

The following week, my younger brother, who looked like me, was on the same turn.

When they had shunted the wagons inside the sidings, he went into the signal box at Swanwick to make a can of tea. He thought the signalman was mad as he would not let him have any hot water and threatened to do him physical harm, all the time ranting about some pen or something.

It was only when my brother mentioned the incident to me that I explained that obviously the signalman had thought my brother was me. Obviously still upset about his bloody pen!

This part of the railway was also near to where a former German prisoner-of-war camp was situated during the Second World War and it was from this camp that German World War II fighter pilot Oberleutenant Franz von Werra escaped on 20th December 1940. Along with three other POWs, von Werra used an escape tunnel to get clear of the camp. Despite his three compatriots soon being recaptured, von Werra decided to continue his bid alone. Following the railway line, he claimed to a friendly locomotive driver that he was downed bomber pilot trying to reach his unit and asked to be taken to the nearest RAF base. At Codnor Park station, a railway clerk, although suspicious, eventually agreed to arrange his transportation to the RAF aerodrome at Hucknall, near Nottingham, where von Werra was recaptured trying to steal a plane. Eventually, he was sent to Canada, where he escaped again before eventually getting back to Germany, via America and then South America. Later a film was made about him and I think it was called 'The One that Got Away', starring Hardy Krüger and based on the 1956 book of the same name by Kendall Burt and James Leasor.

After eventually shunting all the empty wagons into the colliery and all the full ones marshalled ready for the journey back to Toton, the engine and guards van would go on to Ambergate to collect any freight for Toton, stopping on the way back at Swanwick to collect our train.

We would usually arrive back at Toton new sidings where we would unhook, go over the hump and back onto the sheds.

A diesel shunting engine would then go onto the back of the train and push the train over the hump.

Before that, a man would chalk on the side of each wagon its destination code and unhook all the wagons.

As the wagons went over the hump, the code would be read by the man who controlled the points that put each wagon into its correct sidings.

As the wagon ran down the hill the other side of the hump under its own weight, it ran over 'retarders' with which the controllers could apply a braking effect to slow down the wagons so they did not do any damage running into the other previously shunted wagons and so the trains were marshalled for their onward journeys.

The hump still remains today, but the control tower and retarders have all gone as have most of the sidings.

Stanton Gate

Just north of Toton was Stanton Gate sidings which served the nearby Stanton Ironworks. I was on one of the two turns that served the ironworks 24-hours a day, working the night shift. All sorts of traffic went into the works; coal, iron ore, scrap metal and empty wagons ready to be loaded with products from the ironworks, which included spun iron and spun concrete pipes, plus other cast iron products, including tunnel segments.

We had made two trips, into and out of the works and stabled the engine in the sidings while we had our meal break.

Traffic on the Erewash valley line was quite busy and then there was a lull, I remember that suddenly a fitted freight train, hauled by a Peak Class diesel electric locomotive passed the sidings on the up main, while beyond that, on the down goods, was an Austerity 8F with a northbound freight. Immediately there was this awful noise, then silence. My driver immediately said there has been a crash and we had better see what has happened. At the same time the guard and shunter climbed onto the footplate and then ran our engine through an empty road in the sidings, to the south end of the siding.

There in front of us was the wreck of the rear portion of the northbound freight train that had been struck by the southbound fitted freight.

The northbound freight was crossing over the main lines and onto the down slow, when it was stuck by the diesel powered southbound train.

The diesel had all of the front cab crushed after its impact with the northbound freight train, wagons of which lay at all angles around the scene. The wagon that the diesel struck was loaded with concrete gulley sections and ironically, the following wagon contained bandages, among other things, destined for a Boots chemist's store.

The batteries underneath the diesel locomotive were all arcing, giving the impression that the diesel was on fire. While our guard and shunter went to help put out protection, I climbed on board the diesel to see if I could help the crew. Gaining entry via the rear cab, I made my way through the engine room, after first isolating the batteries.

Unfortunately, it was impossible to get into the front cab, where both driver and second man had perished, but we were not to know this for some time, but did suspect it.

The emergency services were called and soon it seemed that this part of the world was alight with blue flashing lights from all the emergency service vehicles responding to the call of a train crash.

Fortunately, because the crash was between two freight trains, the number injured and killed was far lower than if a passenger train had been involved.

The guard on the northbound freight was taken to hospital with his injuries, which were not serious, but sadly the driver and second man on the southbound train were both killed.

Many months later a report on the incident said that after an abundance of fresh air working northwards with a steam engine, in the warm of the cab of a diesel, both crew became drowsy and missed red signals, thus crashing into the crossing freight train.

Lots of people were interviewed, or called to the enquiry, but I was never interviewed, or even asked about it. Despite being so close to the crash and being one of the first on the scene and most importantly, never hearing the bang of a detonator that would have resulted in the diesel passing a red signal at this point.

The signals when showing red automatically placed a detonator on the line, lifting it away when showing a green. The signal had to have the detonators fitted manually.

I was only nineteen at the time and will never forget that fateful night, but still wonder why every avenue was not explored to come to the conclusions the inquiry came to.

This was the very first time I had experienced an emergency, but as fate or circumstances were to dictate, it certainly was not going to be the last.

By daybreak, the scene was swarming with the emergency services, breakdown crews and cranes sent to clean up the mess. They were followed by the permanent way gangs to repair the damaged track work, which was operating again very quickly. Unlike today, when the line would probably have been closed for ages. (This incident can be researched as it is documented, as are all railway accidents.)

You always had to be aware of the dangers that waited for any unguarded moment, which are still present on today's railways, perhaps even more so with increased speeds and quieter trains.

One night at Toton, a driver was hit and killed by a train near Toton centre signalbox while he was making his way to the engineman's cabin. Another Toton driver was killed when he was crushed to death in the cab of his diesel near Peterborough, when he ran into the back of another train while working a train of power station fly ash to Fletton. These and other accidents served to remind everyone that railways were dangerous places.

Wellingborough

Life carried on and I continued to work on all the different local jobs, with the odd trips further afield. I well remember being called up to be the fireman on one of Toton's lodging turns to Wellingborough. We worked our train to Wellingborough, took our engine onto Wellingborough shed and then proceeded to the nearby lodging house, where you could have a meal. We went to the local chip shop, then a pub for a beer, before going to sleep and then working a turn back to Toton the next day.

At one time, railway lodging houses were fairly common, but died out with the end of steam, or shortly after.

The house at Wellingborough was a big house overlooking the railway, between the locomotive depot and the station.

The smell of overcooked cabbage from the kitchen area was always drifting around the lodging house, as meals were cooked around the clock and even the dormitory area smelled of it.

One was given a very small room, consisting of single bed, small bedside cabinet and a copy of Gideon's Bible. More like a cell than a room, but the walls were much thinner and every sound could be heard. It was like being in a communal room and being a light sleeper, the snoring from other parts ensured me a sleepless night. I hated lodging and to this day, I don't sleep at all well away from home.

The smell of cabbage and very limited menu, or rather lack of a menu, more take it or leave it, ensured that many crews cooked their own food at the lodge, or depending on what time of day it was, went to the local chip shop. There were no other fast food outlets at this period, so local chippies were the only source of food.

On regular turns, the driver, fireman and guard would sometimes plan their meal in advance and although the following story was not my experience, it is one that went around the mess room at Toton.

The Toton to Wellingborough night lodging turn was via Melton Mowbray and Corby. The train was put inside a loop to allow the passing of a passenger train and finally came to a stop at the signals.

No. 41947, the only passenger engine permanently based at Toton, used as the shed shunting engine and looked after by a regular crew. This locomotive was first used on the branch line from Ilkeston Junction to Ilkeston Town.

Britannia Class No. 70020 *Mercury*, stationed at Toton for working the double-headed fully fitted coal test trains that ran from Toton to London.

Britannia Class No. 70020 *Mercury* and the dynamometer coach test train at Toton, with No. 70023 *Venus* bringing up the rear.

Double-headed Standard Class 9Fs at Wellingborough with the Down test train to Toton.

Standard Class 9 No. 92153 pilots another Class 9, again at Wellingborough on the Down test train to Toton.

Black 5 No. 45231 runs light engine into Loughborough.

Black 5 No. No. 44767 with Stevenson link motion leaving Rothly with a northbound freight.

I accelerate *Blue Peter* away from Quorn Heading south.

B1 Class No. 61264 at Nottingham Victoria station, taking water before leaving for Skegness with a summer excursion. *(Photograph courtesy Bill Reed)*

Return to the footplate on Black 5 No. 44932 at Butterley.

No. 61264 Leaves Derby station on a special to Buxton.

No. 61264 gets underway from Derby station.

Author during filming for a children's television programme.

Blue Peter passes the post office collecting and pick up apparatus near to Quorn station as it passes with a southbound freight. *(Photograph John East)*

Class A4 No. 60007 *Sir Nigel Gresley* heads a southbound express passing Class N2 No. 69523 heading north at Swithland.

A warm day on the footplate of Jubilee class No. 45593 *Kolhapur* at Loughborough. This engine is now on display at Barrow Hill.

Sir Nigel Gresley waits to come off shed at Loughborough.

Black 5 No. 44767 heads a northbound freight approaching Loughborough.

Allen Grice (ex-Annesley fitter) on the footplate of Butler Henderson as it has its last steaming at Loughborough before return to the National Railway Museum at York (now on loan at Barrow Hill).

Stapleford firemen tackle what was my first house fire as firemen from Long Eaton struggle with their new type helmets in 1966-67.

A view from the rear of our appliance at the same house fire; the pump was front mounted.

A cow trapped in soft mud with a sling around it as we attempt to slowly release the animal. The sling could only be attached by myself and the fireman in the photo getting into the mud with the cow and feeding the sling underneath its belly.

Finally released after about two hours, I stand to the right with one of my leggings pushed up to the top of one boot, but notice I an still wearing my tie (must maintain standards!).

Staplefords pump LRR 999, in which I passed my Fire Service driving test,
standing near Lace Webb spring factory at Sandiacre
during a hydrant testing day.

After a fatal RTA involving a petrol tanker, crews from Dunkirk and West
Bridgford stand by as petrol is burned off from the ditches adjacent to the A453.

Outline of No. 61264.

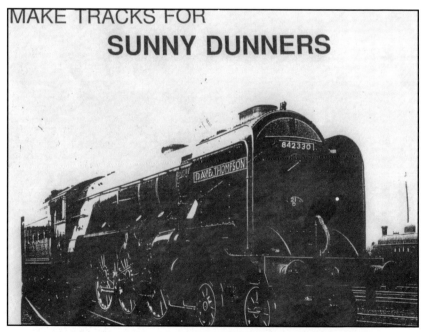

Poster made up to advertise my retirement from the Fire Serve
(the locomotive's number was my Fire Service number!).

Later on the crew planned to have fried steak and boiled new potatoes when they reached the lodging house at Wellingborough.

Beside the loop were some allotments, full of the new season's produce, so why not send the fireman down to the allotments in the dark and pick some fresh vegetables to accompany the potatoes?

Clambering down in the dark, the fireman was filling his bag, when he became aware of the presence of someone very close.

"Who's that?", said that a voice from out the darkness.

The fireman, thinking he would be sacked for theft, swung a sweet left hook in the direction of the voice, feeling the pain as he made a connection with something. With that, he quickly made his way back onto the footplate, just as a passenger train was passing, explaining his agitation to the driver. With that, they both began praying that they would soon have the road. The signal turning to green, their prayers were answered and with a short whistle they were on their way.

As soon as the train came to a stand at Wellingborough, the shunter uncoupled the train and they took the engine onto the shed, before making their way to the lodging house and making a start on the meal and waiting for the guard to arrive.

The guard, when he finally arrived, was sporting a huge black eye.

"Sorry", said the driver, "Have I given you a rough ride?"

"No, nothing like that", the guard replied, "When we were put inside at the loop, I decided to steal some onions for our meal and when I got there, the allotment holder was waiting for me. He hit me and I ran back to the train, Luckily, we got the road and away we went, so he was not able to catch me".

The driver and fireman looked at each other sheepishly, but no one spoke a word. The guard still does not know to this day the truth about who hit him, but he could never understand, whenever the subject came up, why the driver and firemen would break out into laughter.

Another reason to remember the lodging turns occurred when I bought myself a brand new racing bicycle to make my daily round trip from home.

The caller up had delivered the slip to my home changing my turn to a lodging one to Wellingborough. Someone obviously knew of this because while I was away, they stole my new push bike, which was never recovered and I vowed never to have a new one again. In fact, the next thing I purchased was a motorcycle, not a new one, but I did buy a new lock and chain to protect my investment.

The demise of steam was not really thought about too much, even with more and more diesel locomotives starting to appear, mainly on shunting work in the marshalling yards, where there had been a few diesels for a long time, but especially on the passenger express trains. The local trains were also having the steam locomotives replaced by diesel multiple units (DMUs), but at Toton where all our work was freight, diesel power had not yet had much effect.

However, it all seemed to happen so quickly!

One of the first events brought on by the diesels was the closing of many smaller locomotive sheds and later most of the remaining steam sheds.

Some men took early retirement, but others transferred to other sheds, including Toton. If these men were senior, it resulted in Toton men being knocked back in seniority and so there was some resentment, especially among the next batch of firemen due to be passed for driving. Some of who had been on the shovel for over 25 years!

I well remember Kirkby in Ashfield, Westhouses, Annesley, Colwick and even Market Harborough footplate crews transferring to Toton.

Nearly the end of steam

The end of steam came very quickly and as the production of diesel locomotives rapidly accelerated, steam was pensioned off.

Toton had a new depot built to service and repair a large number of diesel locomotives and at that time was the largest depot in Europe.

The first diesels to appear on the main line at Toton were of various classes. Some of the first to come to Toton were the Class 44 Sulzers, numbered D1-D10. All had worked on the West Coast Main Line on passenger work, before being transferred to Toton to haul freight trains. One of these, D3 I think, was the last to arrive after some modifications. Breakdowns were very common in the early days in all the different classes of engines, but considering the mileage and their availability, overall they were a great success.

The biggest problem for diesel locomotives at Toton, or any freight depot, was how to stop a freight train. Most of the rolling stock at this time was made up of unbraked and loose-coupled wagons, the only brake being the one on the locomotive. A very heavy and long freight train takes a long time to be brought to a stop, especially when operated at a greater speed.

There were reports that the heat generated by the cast iron brake blocks on the tyres of the diesels caused the tyres to become detached from the wheels. I personally never saw this, but it was quite common to see the tyres glowing cherry red while under braking. This also led to fires in the locomotives.

The answer at the time was to build brake tenders. These were constructed on double-bogle wagons, resembling very low tanker-type wagons, filled with concrete and with vacuum brakes fitted. These would be attached to the locomotive and provided extra breaking effort. They could be either behind the locomotive, or propelled in front of the locomotive and on some trains, two brake tenders would be used further increasing the braking capacity.

As far as I know, none of these brake tenders survived into preservation.

Later on experiments were carried out using brake blocks made up of a composite material, but with these drivers had to break even earlier than normal to stop where required. They did not find much favour with the crews, who had little confidence in them.

As new rolling stock was built, it was all braked, air brakes replacing the vacuum brakes and some of this vacuum-braked stock is still in existence today.

Where did these diesels leave the fireman? He was still rostered, because occasionally you would be given a steam engine to work a train, but these occurrences became increasingly rare and then only due to the failure of a diesel. There were no spare diesels available at this period, but perhaps there was a rundown steam locomotive that needed to be worked back to its home depot in the north.

At the start of dieselisation, all the trains were double manned, then gradually they became single manned, only being double manned at night times, or when brake tenders were being propelled in front of the diesel.

When the brake tenders went the way of the steam engines, then all turns were single manned.

Since my bicycle had been stolen and I had bought my first motorcycle, one of my interests was racing motorcycles, my spare time being taken up by watching this exciting sport, whenever I could.

I was married with a son, wife and mortgage, so could not afford to race motorcycles myself, but a mate who worked at a motorcycle dealers, raced them. One day I was asked to go along as a spectator and I was immediately hooked, as during a day practising, I was allowed the chance to have a go. Within a short time I was lapping with the fast boys and even beating some of them. I even managed to fall off a few times, but without any lasting injuries.

The dealer was impressed, especially when he learned it was the first time that I had ever raced motorcycles.

The outcome was that he offered me the chance to race on his machinery and without thought of my new family and mortgage, I grabbed the chance.

Without his sponsorship, I would never have had this chance. The dealer had tried solo racing himself, but was not competitive, so he decided to try his hand at motorcycle sidecar scrambling and who did he decide to use as a passenger? Yes, me!

I was small and fearless, so I fitted his criteria perfectly. Each weekend would see us loading up his van, with the bike and spares necessary for the weekend and off to the venue.

As we improved, we were starting to become known, taking on the top riders in our area. Then, one day we took the lead with one lap to go, maybe we were going too fast, or maybe we got too exited, because the next thing I remember was hitting the ground very hard and seeing the motorcycle and sidecar coming through the air to land on top of me.

Winded and with both body and pride bruised, we both were taken to the first aid post.

I had injured my left arm and was unable to race for the rest of the day.

Next day, I had to book sick from the railway and after a visit to the hospital, I was found to have a broken left wrist.

Not good news, as I had no injury insurance and a family and mortgage.

So, my racing career ended almost as soon as it had begun. My regular driver visited me and told me to start back to work as soon as possible and that if we had a steam engine, he would do the firing and let me do the driving. This was good, but I had to get the plaster cast off first and then see the railway doctor before being allowed to start back to work.

As soon as the plaster was removed, I arranged to see the doctor. My arm was pale and withered and very painful, but I needed some wages.

Without even examining my weak arm, which was obviously not up to doing any job, never mind one of a fireman, although I would be alright on a diesel, the doctor, luckily for me, said, "Well, if you think you can do the job, then start back".

On the Monday, I started back to work after 12 weeks off with my regular driver, then on the Thursday the caller up brought me notice that my duty had changed. I was on the Ashfordby to York fitted iron ore train. My driver did not sign for York at this time, so I knew that I would have a different driver, no problem because we would have a Class 45 Sultzer engine Peak diesel for the trip to York and back.

These fitted iron ore trains were very heavy trains, run at fast speeds with the diesels working very hard. The only other engines that could maintain this speed and effort was the Standard Class 9, the class of locomotive which used to work these trains before the arrival of the diesels. But, it used to be a very hard shift for the fireman, as the drivers had to work the engines very hard to maintain the booked times.

Due to the need for water stops, their paths were often lost and it was normally a 12-hour shift for the crews, before arriving back at Toton.

Signing-on for duty, I met my driver and then we walked to the train crew cabin at Toton Centre signal box, where we met our guard. Cabins similar to this were all over the railway system. Inside would always be found a cast iron kettle on a gas ring, always topped up and always near to boiling, ready for a brew in your tea can.

A telephone was usually fixed to the wall to enable the crew to tell Control that you were there and they in turn would tell you the progress of the train that you were to relieve and the engine number.

Sometimes, they would not have any details yet, which usually meant the train was running late and could result in a long wait.

This is what happened this night and so we made a brew and settled down to wait the call from Control. Eventually, we were informed that our train was running two hours late and were given the engine number. It was the number of a steam locomotive, an Austerity 8F 2-8-0, No. 90295 which was just about the worst engine to have! The only good point was that the 8Fs were free steaming engines, but they were very rough riding at slow speeds, never mind express freight speed and they were not strong enough for these trains.

On top of all this, I had only one good arm - it was not looking good.

Finally, we relieved the crew and set off up the Erewash valley, every shovel full of coal causing me extreme pain and I had to resort to firing using just my right arm.

Our trip was, luckily for me, very slow, as we were kept on the very busy slow line as far as Chesterfield, so I was able to maintain boiler pressure.

Little and often was the key, as I used one arm to both fire the engine and pull forward the coal in the tender. Our journey was all stop start, as we were held everywhere by adverse signals; somebody was obviously looking after me. Not the driver, who had told me that I should not be there if I could not do the job and offered no help at all, despite my pain and stream of swear words as I jarred my left arm.

Arriving at Masboro, we were once again put inside and we had now been on duty for eight hours, with the prospect of many more hours if we worked on to York.

When I told my driver that I was going to telephone Control and ask to be relieved, his reaction was one of anger at the possible loss of so much overtime and he said that he didn't require relief.

Speaking to Control, I asked to be relieved and their reply was that "You're booked to work to York and back and that's what your going to have to do!".

"No", I said, "We are booked a diesel and run at express freight speed. We are doing none of these, so I will not go past Masboro".

At this point, I was joined by the guard who backed my views and also demanded a relief.

Eventually, after a long wait, we were all relieved and told to make our way back to Toton.

Because of the loss of so much overtime, the driver was refused to talk to the guard and myself.

We had by now been on duty for nine hours and still had to get home by passenger train and by the time we did, we had been on duty for twelve hours, four hours overtime.

The York jobs were 10-hour shifts, so we had made more than that anyway.

Next day, both my arms were very sore, but it must have been good physiotherapy, because I never had any problems with my arm again.

The following week, I made it as far as Normanton, again with an Austerity 8F No. 90684, followed the very next day, all the way to York with No. 90417. I was back, but by this time, October 1966, turns on steam engines were very rare.

So, now it was nearly all diesels. At the start, all diesels had a second man as part of the crew, but later on they only required a second man at night.

This resulted in plenty of night work for the firemen/secondmen and I seemed never to see my family, as we seemed to be on permanent nights, although we worked AM duty one week, followed by PM duty the following week.

The catch was the times on duty PM duty 23.59 hrs, or one minute to midnight. The following week AM duty 00.01hrs, or one minute after midnight, so much for bloody days and nights.

It was time to look at other jobs and the Fire Service looked good as it offered glamour and excitement, which was much better than factory work.

I had had a good time on the footplate; it had been a challenge to which I had risen on most occasions, as every fireman struggled at some stage at the end of a shovel.

However, some memories will always be with me.

Steam cleaning the cobbled floor of the engine shed to get rid of the accumulated oil, grease and muck. During this job, usually done by engine cleaners, a junior cleaner's grease top hat was placed on top of an engine whistle and then the whistle was blown, blowing the hat into orbit. When the young man retrieved his hat, he found that the hot steam had shrunk the leather cap lining to less than half size, making it useless. Very funny at that time!

The only way he could obtain a new one was to tell the store-man that his hat had been stolen.

Much of the track renovation work was carried out on Sundays, as this was the day when there was least traffic. This could be very boring work for the engine crews, as sometimes these trains never moved through out the shift after they had arrived at the site of the work.

During one of these days, a guard who was new to the job, came onto the engine to talk to us. During this chat, he was asked were he used to work? "I was an Opera singer", he said to two disbelieving engine crew members.

"Bloody opera singer! What the hell are you doing as a guard?"

"Well, I had a nervous breakdown, was out of work and needed some money", he explained, "The railways are short of guards".

He was a small, thin weedy-looking young man and certainly did not fit our picture of an opera singer, but then standing on the veranda of his guards van, he started to sing, in Italian. A voice that was absolutely stunning filled the air and brought all the work to a standstill, the platelayers joining us as we stared open-mouthed as our guard entertained us.

Absolutely stunning and we had to offer our apologies for not believing him. His performance was brought to a halt by the foreman, who had to complete the job without the distractions of an opera singer.

Codnor Park must have been the only place in the world where for the first and possibly the last time, the railways were brought to a stop by an opera singer. I don't know what ever happened to him, but he did not stay on the railway.

The diesel era saw the engine crews move to a brand new diesel depot at Toton, where everything was clean and bright and so much different to the old steam sheds.

The old steam sheds still saw steam locomotives, but not very often, with just the odd one standing in for a failed diesel.

The job was cleaner all around, with warm cabs, cooking facilities on the engines and you went home clean. What was missing? The teamwork, when against all odds, bad weather, poor coal and a bad steaming engine, the engine crews completed the job satisfaction.

The diesels were masters of their jobs, especially as they became more reliable. They ran for a lot longer without the need for the servicing that the steam engine needed, but they were different and this was progress.

Life with the diesels was certainly easier, especially for the fireman/secondman. All you had to do was observe the signals and check the train, but sometimes, the driver would ask you to go through the engine room to check everything was OK.

Also, you would be allowed to drive on a lot more occasions than on the steam engines, especially with the older drivers.

Toton was the service depot for a great number of diesels, so many turns involving collecting and returning engines to depots where there were no service facilities.

Regularly, we would have to take an engine straight to Derby, or Nottingham stations, to work the London express. We would back on to the train in the platform, then be relieved by the Derby, or Nottingham driver rostered for the turn.

We were normally relieved a few minutes, or sometimes seconds before departure and occasionally intending passengers were shocked when they asked the driver, "Does this train stop at Kettering?"

When they were told, "Sorry, no idea!", the look of panic on their faces can be imagined.

"Well, if the driver doesn't know then, who the hell does?"

These last minute jobs to the stations were usually as a result of another engine failing and it was a good effort by everyone to ensure these trains left on time.

Working what was called a 'spare' turn, my driver and myself sat in the mess room. This was when you signed on duty and covered any emergency that may arise. Sometimes, you never left the shed, but then suddenly, you could be called to work anything.

This particular day, towards the end of our shift, we were called to run a Class 45 Peak diesel to Nottingham Midland station for a London express, where we would be relieved. I was with my regular driver and it was my turn to drive. No problems and we were relieved in the platform at Nottingham. Calling in to Control, we were instructed to go to Nottingham shed to take two Class 2 Sulzers back to Toton.

Reporting to the shed running foreman, we were given the two engine numbers. The two locomotives were already coupled together in tandem, so we had only to start them up and we could be gone (my driver was in a hurry to get back as he had a darts match to go to at his local pub in Long Eaton).

To leave Nottingham shed you had to inform the signalman by means of a plunger, but in our hurry, we decided to drive up to the signalbox and shout our destination to the 'bobby' (signalman).

"Sorry, but there is a diesel coming onto the shed, so you will have to set back", said the bobby. I already had the engines in reverse and proceeded to set back. Bang! Bang! and the movement in the cab told us immediately that we were off the road.

Brakes hard on, we came to a stop and climbed down to look at the damage. The set of points where we had derailed was wrecked, as one engine had gone one way and the other derailed onto the sleepers, breaking all the cast iron chairs of the points.

My fault, as I had forgotten about the catch points in our haste to get off shed, but ultimately my driver's fault, because he was the driver. It would be many hours before anything could be able to get in and out of Nottingham shed, as we had effectively closed it, trapping quite a few passenger engines scheduled to take out express trains.

We were in trouble, up to our armpits, but all my mate could think off was his darts match. Straight to the foreman's office we went and admitted it was our fault entirely. We would submit a full written report to this effect before going off duty. The foreman was impressed with our honesty and told us to catch the next passenger train and make our way back to Toton after my driver told him it was no good us hanging about, while the breakdown train and emergency platelayers were called out.

The report was written while on our way back to Toton, via the passenger train, where we signed off duty and went home. At least, I went home and my driver made his darts match. Because of our admissions of guilt, we both only received cautions for our mishap of closing Nottingham shed before Dr. Beeching closed it forever.

Really, I cannot imagine that this would happen today, with all the rules and regulations that strangle working practices nowadays.

This jogs my memory of other practices in days of steam, namely alcohol. I remember when only sixteen-years-old and on the main line, after being relieved, going straight into a pub and being bought a pint of beer by the driver, before working another train back home. The railways seemed to be run on beer; I remember the shunting engines at Burton-on-Trent carried stone jars of beer on the engine, presumably for the engine crews. Imagine that happening nowadays!

I wonder if there were many incidents on these shunting turns attributed to Burton Beer?

One driver I was rostered with liked his beer more than most and while he had the money, spent nearly all his time off duty in the pub. When the money ran out, he would borrow from his wife, or even me, although to his credit, he always paid his debts on Friday - payday. So, the pattern repeated itself week in week out. He also smoked Capstan Full Strength cigarettes, which were expensive in comparison to Park Drives, or Woodbines.

The key to me knowing he had no money was seeing him light up and smoke a Black Cat cigarette (his wife smoked Black Cat, another strong cigarette, but slightly milder than Capstan Full Strength). He had borrowed cigarettes from his wife because he had no money until payday. Most probably he had also borrowed some money for his beer as well.

He was a small man, not physically able to fire an engine for long. However, he was happy to let me drive, if I did the firing as well, while he smoked and looked out and instructed me how to drive a steam locomotive.

I was quite happy to do this, as I was only a teenager, very fit and pleased at this opportunity. One turn saw us on duty at 1155 a.m. with a Stanier Class 8 2-8-0. We worked empty wagons to a colliery sidings, where we shunted in the empties and made up a train of coal for the south. Then, after eating our snap (food), we would work the train back to Toton.

My driver liked this turn, as he could have a drink before signing on duty.

He would then sit in the fireman's seat, while I was driving and firing the engine.

After arrival at the colliery sidings, he would go to the local pub, or club, while I did the shunting of the empties and formed the train for our return. He would then return to eat his snap and we would work a train back to Toton. Back on the engine shed, he would leave me to dispose of the engine and stable it, while he made out any repair cards that was necessary.

Signing off duty, he would be off like a greyhound to spend the rest of the night in the pub. He retired, without having to convert to diesels, but looked a frail and tired old man, who according to most, would not see too many New Years in retirement. Despite his liking for beer and very strong cigarettes, he outlived most of his cleaner living contemporaries.

During my time with him, he taught me invaluable lessons, on how to work and handle loose-coupled steam trains. This was a very skilful task with a long train of loose-coupled wagons, especially when working over lines badly affected by mining subsidence that resembled a roller coaster rather than a main line. Part of the train, or even different parts, would be going downhill, while the other parts were going uphill. Get it wrong and the couplings would break!

Stopping and starting a loose-coupled train was a skill that took practice, something that could not be learned from a book.

Start off too quickly and you may break a coupling, or even worse injure the guard, who was suddenly accelerated from zero to 12/15mph in seconds, with the result that he was thrown across the guard's van and possibly injured. This happened on numerous occasions with steam engines, but more so with diesels.

When braking, if the brakes on the engine were not used cautiously, gently allowing the wagons to buffer up to each other before heavier braking, the guard again could be injured by the sudden deceleration.

Some of our trains from Wellingborough to Toton had up to 97 empty loose-coupled wagons on and this called for very skilful driving.

After a year with him as his regular fireman, I changed links and became the fireman for another driver. What a change, he was a lay preacher who didn't even swear and in my view should never have been an engine driver. In my year or so with him, I don't recall driving on more than a couple of occasions. Frustrating at first, but I soon got used to just firing again after my previous driving experience with my previous driver.

I tried my hardest to make him swear, but apart from the word 'blinking', he never did. A nice man really, who was not really suited, or confident out on the main line, reflected in the fact that his route card did not allow him to go far from Toton.

One day as we sat on our engine, we were informed that a diesel had failed on a passenger train and we would have to go on the front and work it on to Nottingham. I was quite exited at the prospect of a Stanier 8F 2-8-0 on the front of this express. Not my mate! He reported that he was just about to report that we had a tender axle-box running hot and could not do this work.

We had never had a 'hot box' and I was so upset that we were not going to work the express, that from then on I really lost all respect for him and luckily moved on to another link shortly afterwards.

Three brothers all firemen at Toton did not make us unique. Three other brothers - the Walkers - were already at Toton, although only one made it to driver; one worked in the stores and the other one was a fire raiser.

They all had the nickname of 'Buck', why I never knew. Buck the driver, was married to a woman who was confined to a wheelchair. Because of this he would swap his main line turns with young drivers rostered onto shed duties, so he knew when he would be home.

He was a man who liked a practical joke, so was liked by most of the young firemen.

On days when he had been unable to swap his turns, he had a trick that he would use to ensure he had a good run.

Passing a signalbox he would don a bowler hat and stand so as to be seen by the signalman.

The signalman seeing him would report that an inspector was riding on this particular train. This usually ensured the train would have a good run where possible.

Very often this ploy would work and I remember one day when he had used it, being stopped eventually and being asked by the signalman had we an inspector on the footplate? "No, not now", he replied, "He got off earlier". As far as I know, he was never caught out. Apart from the bowler hat, he also carried a big pair of rubber monkey's ears.

When we had worked to Wellingborough or somewhere and were sent home by passenger train because there was no return work, he would get onto the train wearing these ears, sit down and just stare in front of him. He could sit and not make any facial movement all the way home and the reactions from the passengers varied from laughter to pretending that they had not noticed.

When I was a passed cleaner and then a young fireman, many turns involved what was called spare.

Reporting for duty, you were usually sent to the canteen until you were required. As a crew, you could be tasked with preparing an engine, or some shunting in the shed yard, or you could be sent out on the main line on a special job. Mostly, you would be sent out to relieve a crew who had asked for relief as they were already on overtime.

It was common in the early sixties for trains for Toton sidings to be queuing one behind the other for miles, especially if there was a problem, such as a derailment in the sidings. So, we were sent out to relieve these crews, sometimes hardly moving before we eventually also required relief.

These were boring days, but days when lots of cribbage was played by the driver and firemen, very often watched by the guard from the train in front, as we used his guard's van which was more comfortable than the footplate. Of course, from time to time we would have to check that our fire was still alight and there was water in the boiler.

Many hours were spent waiting in various locomens' cabins in various places.

Trent station had a large locomen's room, where crews could wait hours waiting to relieve trains. So many crews from Toton went to and from Trent station, that a regular bus service operated to and from Toton to Trent station and even through the night, the railway bus would be there.

Inside any locomen's room, there would be a large cast iron kettle permanently boiling, with the notice 'One out one in' chalked onto the kettle. This ensured that you only had to wait seconds for boiling water and this way, passing trains could pick up a can of water for their tea.

A feature I remember at Trent, was that a heavy timber table had carved into its top, a shove halfpenny board, which waiting crews played to pass the time. The phone would then ring and control would tell the crews where their trains were, or their progress when running late. Late running trains would very often ask for relief at Trent, knowing that crews were always there and there was transport available back to Toton.

These rooms or cabins were replicated all over the rail network, but have now gone, along with Trent and many other stations.

These stories were in the days when we only worked steam, as the drivers in the last stories, retired before having to convert from steam to diesel traction.

The job had completely changed and each day was pretty much the same as the previous one. No two steam engines were the same, so everyday brought a different challenge. Even if you had the same engine, a different driver with different driving styles, changed everything for the fireman and for the guard on a loose-coupled train.

The very last steam locomotive I worked on British Railways was Standard Class 5 No. 73039, which was on 30th January 1967. I cannot remember where from, or on what train, but my diary records that I worked the engine to Derby, but sadly I did not record any other details.

I only found some old diaries when I moved home and looking through these, I found that sometimes I had recorded the jobs that I had worked, sometimes with the engine number and sometimes even recorded the driver's name. Overall, I was not a very good diarist, keeping my entries to the very basics.

During my last days working steam, I seemed to have made a brief record of the last steam locomotives I fired and I list them below with their dates:

05/1/1965	Stanier 8F 2-8-0 No. 48146 Toton to Wath
07/1/1965	Austerity 2-8-0 No. 90149 Toton to Parkgate
12/1/1965	Stanier 5F 4-6-0 No. 44661 Toton to Foleshill
13/1/1965	Stanier 8F 2-8-0 No. 48538 Toton to Foleshill
18/1/1965	Austerity 2-8-0 No. 90509 Toton to Normanton
20/1/1965	Stanier 8F 2-8-0 No. 48126 Toton to Normanton
09/2/1965	Stanier 8F 2-8-0 No. 48621 Stanton Gate
10/2/1965	Austerity 2-8-0 No. 90474 Toton to Falkirk
10/2/1965	Austerity 2-8-0 No. 90084 Falkirk to Toton
14/2/1965	Stanier 8F 2-8-0 No 48530 Stanton Gate
16/2/1965	Thompson B1 4-6-0 No. 61094 Toton to Trafford Park
17/2/1965	Stanier 2-6-0 No. 43033 Toton to Trafford Park
17/2/1965	Austerity 2-8-0 No 90558 Trafford Park to Toton
18/2/1965	Standard 9F 2-10-0 No. 92161 Toton to Trafford Park
08/3/1965	Stanier 8F 2-8-0 No. 48394 Toton to Leeds
15/3/1965	Austerity 2-8-0 No. 90315 Toton to Masboro
18/3/1965	Standard 9F 2-10-0 No. 92179 Toton to Masboro

I did not record any other steam turns recorded from 18 March 1965 until 7 October 1965

During this time, my son was born and I had eight weeks off work with a broken arm, the result of a crash while racing motorcycles!

7/10/1965	Austerity 2-8-0 No. 90295 Toton to Masboro (fired with one hand)
2/6/1966	Jubilee 4-6-0 No. 45694 *Bellarophan* (No record of journey)
22/7/1966	Austerity 2-8-0 No. 90429 Masboro
23/7/1966	Stanier 8F No. 48143 Toton to Masboro

It was obvious that the diesels were the future and there was nothing much to look forward to, except that we went further afield.

The first Peaks built (Class 44 Nos. D1-D10) were then transferred to Toton to see out their time on freight trains and remained until they were scrapped, or in one case preserved to run on heritage railways.

I think the last to arrive was No. D3, which was used for some experimental work and arrived with a more powerful engine than the others in the class.

One thing that did change, however, was the number of times you were allowed to drive. Many an older driver, who wouldn't have allowed you to drive a steam locomotive, were quite happy to sit in the second man's seat in a diesel and let you drive.

Steam was still used even in the diesels, as they were fitted with static boilers to heat up the coaches of the passenger trains.

Trained in the different types of static boilers, the fireman/secondman had to operate them in winter to prevent them freezing up. No problem on a passenger train, but on a freight train, we would open the steam heating pipe to atmosphere between the engine and the train. Many times this caused all sorts of people, including signalmen, to report that a train was on fire, especially if the boiler safety valve opened on the roof of the diesel.

With single manning rapidly approaching and the closure of many steam sheds, the railways had many surplus footplate men. So, the prospect of being passed for driving seemed to be getting further away. It was time to look to the future and I could not see any on the railways for me.

Then, a chance! A foreman's job was to become vacant at Toton and I thought I would apply for it. This was unheard of, as usually only drivers with many years experience would traditionally apply for these jobs.

Interviews were held and I had many test situations given to me, all of which I passed and I reached the final selection, only to be told that while competent, they considered that perhaps I was too young for the job of foreman.

I then looked elsewhere and decided my future was away from the railway. I already was a member of the Nottinghamshire Fire Service as a retained fireman and when I saw a job advertised for a fireman at the local Ironworks I applied. On being offered the job, I handed in my notice at Toton, probably thinking at the time that this would be the end of my connections with the railways.

So, I left the railways for the local Stanton ironworks, a place where my father worked and where as a fireman, I had worked freight into and out of the works.

Crossing the line from making fires to putting them out, I started my new job at the Fire Station.

Steam was also in decline at the ironworks, the Andrew Barclay saddle-tank locomotives used in works standing silent and rusting, waiting for the scrap man's cutting torch.

I was not to know that within a few years time, iron production would cease at Stanton Ironworks and another industry passed on into history.

I did not stay to the end of iron production at the works, as I wanted some security and the County Fire service offered, that even if I had to take a wage drop.

Chapter Four

The Fire Service

Suddenly, I had changed my life! From making fires, I was now putting them out, hence the title of this book - 'Both Sides of the Fire'.

I joined the Nottinghamshire Fire Service as a retained (part time) fireman in 1966 at Stapleford, while still working as a fireman for British Railways at Toton. Consequently, all the time when I was not on duty on the railway, I would be on call for the Fire Service.

After joining the Fire Service and passing a medical, work permitting, I was told to report every Monday night for training and also to report to the fire station on hearing the siren. The siren was situated on the roof of the then Carr Fastener Factory on Nottingham Road, Stapleford.

Initially, I was not issued any uniform, which I would receive after completing my initial training course and then I would be allowed to ride on the fire engine to emergencies.

My first fire was a grass fire on the football ground of the Old Cross Dye works, adjacent to the railway line near Stapleford and Sandiacre railway station. More than likely, the cause being recorded as a spark from a passing locomotive, which was a common cause in the days of steam!

Despite not having done my initial training at this time, on one callout the fire crew was short of one man, so I was told to grab a fire kit from one of the pegs in the fire station, jump aboard the fire engine and "Do as you are told!".

This fire was quickly put out using beaters and the hose reel jet from the appliance.

Little did I know that this would be the first of thousands of calls over the next 31 years.

Having left the railways and joined the Fire and Safety Dept. of Stanton Ironworks, I was still a retained fireman.

Working at Stanton Ironworks as a fireman was very varied, because as well as being a fireman, you were also a safety man and an ambulance man.

They still used Andrew Barclay saddle-tank steam locomotives on the miles of internal rail networks inside the vast ironworks and I was especially fascinated with the engines that had a steam crane built onto them. However, like the steam locomotives on British Railways, these would only last for a short time before the diesels took over.

We had two fire appliances and two ambulances and the job involved working shift work around the clock, which was no different to what I had been doing previously, but the work was very different.

We were very busy for a works brigade, attending at least one fire every shift, mainly due to loading red-hot pig iron ingots into wooden-bodied railway wagons.

The five iron furnaces always provided plenty of work, both for the fire appliances and also for the ambulances. The work was hot, heavy and dangerous and the ambulances were always out dealing with both minor and also major accidents and illnesses.

Most of these were fairly minor, but occasionally the more serious accident would happen.

The first time I had to take a body to the mortuary will always remain in my memory. I had to drive the ambulance, with just the corpse on the stretcher in the back for company, to the small local mortuary where I was to meet up with the police constable who was the Coroner's Officer and in charge of placing the body into the mortuary. Colleagues had told me that if it was an experienced police officer, he would tell me it was my job to strip the body of clothing before placing it onto the slab, or trolley. As this apparently was not part of my duties, I was advised only to do it if I felt I wanted to help. After a nerve-wracking wait for the constable outside the mortuary, he finally arrived, a young constable who was as nervous as me. However, luck was with us both! When we explained to the council worker who arrived with the keys that this was our first corpse, he willingly helped us to complete the grisly task and complete all the formalities in a very small mortuary, that on this particular day was absolutely full of bodies.

It's amazing how long you can hold your breath for, although the man from the council he'd done this job many times and did not notice the smell.

Due to the mortuary being particularly busy, it was quite a problem fitting in another body on a stretcher into the small place. As the policeman and me pushed the stretcher inside, we accidentally bumped into another trolley containing a covered body, the hand and arm from this body falling across our stretcher. The council man immediately said, "Take your hand off him - you sex maniac!".

Obviously, this particular body was a female and the one we had brought in a male, a sick remark maybe, but it helped to ease the situation for two nervous newcomers to the mortuary.

While at British Steel at Stanton, I joined the works fire brigade competition team.

Contests were held at many different venues around the country for various drills for the fire teams, Stanton having a good reputation as quality competitors and winning many prestigious trophies and cups.

The blue ribbon event was a one-man drill, the fireman having to place his equipment on the ground inside a marked square. When the starting gun sounded, he opened the hydrant pit, fixed the hydrant, ran out one length of hose, fitted the nozzle and placed the nozzle into a clip which stopped the clock.

All the equipment was then checked by the judges, time being added for any incorrect fitting or twists in the hose.

My first and last one man hose drill was at the football ground at Gainsborough. The gun went off and I sprang into action, hydrant lid off, hydrant shipped, hose connected and ran out, nozzle in and fitted into the timing clip. A hose without a twist, could this be a new world record? The time was certainly inside the old record. As the judge removed the nozzle from the clip, it became disconnected from the hose and so with the resulting penalty, I had lost the world record.

Eventually, British Steel at Stanton gave out hints that some plants would need to be closed, as they were losing so much money. As it became obvious that this job might not last forever, I decided to apply to join the County Fire Service, full time.

The wages were less, but I would retire at 55-years old and it was a job I loved doing.

I had become a retained fireman while I was still on the railway, being introduced to the service by another fireman at Toton, who was already a member, joining in 1966 at Stapleford, where the fire station was on Warren Avenue.

You were paid a retaining fee for the time you were on call, extra pay for when you were called out. A large bell was fitted in your house and the local air raid siren would sound when there was a fire call. Training took place for two hours every Monday night and you were also sent away for weekend training with the full-time firemen, before being allowed to turn out to incidents. Breathing apparatus and driving courses followed.

During my time as a retained fireman, I was to attend all sorts of calls ranging from grass, chimney, house, factory and vehicle fires, to the special service calls for the release of trapped people, or animals.

One rescue of a cow trapped in clinging mud, remains a memory, both for the difficulty of its rescue and the state we were all in due to the mud and water. The cow had gone to have a drink of water from a trough situated at the bottom of an embankment of a motorway. During the years, the cattle had worn away the ground, so that the trough was in a small basin. The water had overflowed over some time, so that the ground was very muddy. The cow had become stuck in the mud and the more it tried to free itself, the more deeply it became trapped in the mud. Only the cow's head was free when we arrived.

Only after much digging and fixing a harness under the cow and the use of two winches to lift and pull at the same time, were we able to release the very tired and shocked cow. The operation took over three hours and used three fire appliances and crews, who were also very tired and very muddy.

Another early fire I attended was a huge factory fire at a tea warehouse in Long Eaton, Derbyshire, where a full time fireman from Long Eaton rescued trapped workers from above the height of his ladder, a brave rescue for which he was later decorated. This was one of the largest fires that I would attend in my entire career and was just a stone throw from my former railway depot at Toton.

I remember being there and watching in amazement as the walls collapsed, even falling onto adjacent buildings, but luckily I don't think anyone was injured during the fire, or during the following days it took to completely extinguish the fire and make everything safe.

My first house fire involved me using breathing apparatus for the first time at a real fire, as opposed to a training scenario.

Although some memories have started to fade, I remember well the first time I was the appliance driver and drove to a real incident, with the excitement making my right foot tremble as I held the accelerator down to the floor.

I remained a retained fireman until I joined the full time service in 1972.

Most firemen at this time joined for the job satisfaction, not the wages, but a pension at 55 was attractive, even if we paid a lot into the pension scheme from our then meagre wages.

Usually, on joining the full time Fire service, you were sent straight to a training school for 14 weeks where you were instructed and passed out in the basics. However, because I had been a retained fireman for six years and because I was trained in wearing breathing apparatus and a was brigade driver, it was to be six months before I was sent to Leicester City Fire Brigade for my basic training, which was compulsory for all firemen.

I had a great advantage over most of the recruits, as I was already familiar with all the equipment, so the practical side was easier for me. The theoretical was different and we all had a lot to learn, as much of it was as new to me as to the other recruits

On the practical side, hook ladders were certainly new to me and everyone else on the course. We did not use them in Nottinghamshire and many of the other brigades had phased them out. Training schools still kept them as confidence boosters, or confidence destroyers, depending on the individual.

These ladders were used to climb vertically up the face of a building, the only thing holding the ladder in place being a large hook, which rested on the windowsill. You would hook the ladder on the window sill above you, climb the ladder to the window sill, sit astride the sill and then repeat the process to the next floor above and so on. While climbing the ladder, you had to lean away from the building to ensure that the hook did not move. Not to bad at the first floor, but it needed confidence at the fourth, or fifth floors.

I remember some recruits would be physically sick when the instructor said the next drill would be hook ladders, some even leaving the course as they could not come to terms with them. Shortly afterwards, they were banned completely.

The last week of the training was spent training for the passing out parade, held in front of relatives and local invited dignitaries at Leicester Central Fire station.

The top three recruits were awarded special prizes and I was lucky enough to be one of the three. I still have the books about the fire service, but they are now outdated by the advances in the modern fire and rescue service.

Looking back now, the three months spent at Leicester were very good. However, it was a strain for some being away from family and friends, when none of us had much money, so could not afford to be out at night all the time.

Some of the recruits found evening work as doormen in the city's night clubs, which was much against the rules that said we had to be in our lodgings at 10.30 p.m.

After a night out, the walk back to the fire station where we lived was along a street frequently used by the oldest profession in the world. Hastings Street was where the ladies would ask if we wanted anything?

"Only if it's free!", we would reply.

Their response would be just two words!

Back to my station, West Bridgford, Nottingham, where I would have to complete two years probation and continual study to complete my training and final acceptance into the Brigade, although the training and study never ended through out my career.

Most of the time the general public were most grateful and supportive of the Fire Service, but like most things, there are always exceptions.

One evening, we were called to a house fire in West Brigford, Nottingham. I was a member of a four-man team of breathing apparatus wearers sent in to locate and fight the fire, searching for people, or animals that may be trapped in the smoke and fire.

The fire was located and extinguished and then the house vented to rid it of smoke.

After returning to the Fire station, the Office-in-Charge (OIC) was informed from Fire Control that the owner had contacted the police to report that a very valuable diamond bracelet had been stolen, or gone missing, from one of the bedrooms and that the police were on the way to the Fire Station to take statements from all involved with the fire.

After the questioning of all the crews by these detectives, I was recalled to be re-interviewed.

The owners said that the bracelet had been in the bedroom that only I had been inside and where I had gone to open the windows to help vent the building.

The detectives wanted to know why I could not describe the décor and contents of the room;, my reason being that my only intention was to open the windows.

Yes, I could remember a bed, but could not recall any other detail. Anyway, they did not appear to be satisfied, returning on other occasions to further question me.

I don't suppose that I helped too much, appearing very flippant about the incident, but after more visits it began to be appear threatening, especially as I knew I was innocent.

I had not seen or taken anything in my life and was convinced neither had my colleagues.

Between us, we had decided that this was probably because a false insurance claim was pending.

Eventually, a different fire crew was dispatched to the house, where all the rubbish was sifted through, along with the rubbish bins, but still no bracelet.

The police then started to question the homeowners more thoroughly and a few days later, as if by magic, the bracelet was found in another part of the house.

This had been a very uncomfortable time for all the crew and quite a fright for me, as I realised the police initially suspected me.

As far as I know, no apologies were ever received for this slur on both our names and the Fire Service; a very early lesson that you have to take note of all things in life.

On a lighter note, all firemen would take part in fund raising for the Fire Service National Benevolent Fund, with stations competing for a trophy for the highest amount of money raised per head of the station staff.

This charity does a fantastic job, helping all serving firemen, their wives and children, plus retired firemen and their families in their time of need through injuries, illness, convalescence and rehabilitation.

All of which costs an enormous amount of money to run.

Returning to duty after my days off, I learned that our station had decided to help to raise funds by producing a pantomime.

Station personnel would do everything needed to produce a production that would entertain all who come to see it.

Oh! I nearly forgot, in my absence, I had been cast in the role of Simple Simon.

Many hours were put in both on duty and off duty to make and paint scenery and the costumes required. In fact, there were hundreds of jobs that were shared by firemen, cooks, cleaners and office staff, including families, to prepare for this to be a success.

A script was produced by a good friend of mine - Colin Shakespeare - who was a Sub Officer at Beeston Fire Station and had previous experience writing and producing pantomime at Beeston Fire Station.

After many delays, the final script was finished and distributed to the cast, who then set about learning their lines and rehearsing the masterpiece.

I was handed my script on a single piece of paper and to my horror read 'AD LIB', 'AD LIB'.

I had never before had any desire, or the nerve, to appear on any stage, so was immediately filled with both horror, fear and trepidation as to the outcome of the foolhardy decision to take part in the pantomime.

Rehearsals never seemed to improve the situation and with the opening night approaching like an express train, stage fright reached unprecedented levels, even amongst the actors with written lines. Mix this with illness to key people and staff and we never ever thought we would complete this mammoth undertaking.

The venue for our pantomime was going to be the Day Centre at the rear of West Bridgford Fire Station, kindly offered to us by their management as they had a large hall and stage.

Obviously, one performance would be for their enjoyment, we hoped, the other audiences made up of the paying public and some performances for the handicapped and pensioners.

Local businesses kindly donated gifts, so that presents could be given to everyone that attended.

Finally, the opening night arrived and the cast was to found enjoying a few drinks at a local bar, to steady the nerves that everyone suffered.

It's all well and good rescuing people from dangerous situations, but standing on a stage wearing a stupid outfit, sucking a giant dummy and telling a audience, packed to the rafters, that you are Simple Simon, takes nerves of steel and about half a bottle of scotch, if I remember right.

Just before curtain call there was panic, one of the leading actors lost his voice completely, due to illness or fright, or both.

To the rescue came Colin our writer, director and producer, who would stand in for the part. Unfortunately, due standing in at the last minute, he did not know the precise lines, so carried a clipboard with the words pasted on it.

Everything was working like clockwork, until Colin reached his first line, raising his clipboard to his eyes!

"B*****ds", he exclaimed.

Someone had erased all his lines.

Everybody in the place, even the audience had been told, all except poor old Colin.

But, as the writer of the pantomime, he was able to make up his lines as he went along, which added to the fun.

A hugely successful first night got even better the more we performed it and also resulted in taking the pantomime on the road.

One place we were invited to perform was a large mental hospital where I refused to go on stage and announce myself as Simple Simon. It was during this performance that Colin struck back, after having his script sabotaged.

Between scene changes, Colin, who had a fine singing voice, would entertain the audience with a medley of songs. Out of the blue, he encouraged the audience to demand a solo song from Simple Simon, knowing full well that I could not sing to save my life, let alone sing solo to about two hundred people.

Finally, after being dragged on stage by other cast members, the pianist asked what song I wanted and what key should he play in? Lucky for me, I had overdosed on my stage fright medicine and was able to complete my stint as the world's worst pub singer, although I am still frightened by Karaoke to this day.

Thanks for the memories Colin.

Firemen all over the country do many different things to raise money, but the pantomime was the hardest and most pleasurable thing that I took part in.

Others ranged from walking around Nottingham in full kit and wearing breathing apparatus to set a world record for the longest distance in this kit, probably now beaten. Also, climbing a set of ladders to the height of Mount Everest in a day, again set in the Market Square in Nottingham. The more mundane included door-to-door collections, or even standing outside the B&Q store with collecting tins (incidentally, the last one raised the most money for the least time and effort).

The object of all this was to raise money for various charities, but mainly for the Fire Brigade National Benevolent Fund, who could not do such a brilliant job without the commitment from both the Fire Service and the generous donations of the British public.

Chapter Five

The day the world caught on fire

In the early part of my service in the Fire Brigade, Sundays were always different; the mornings being spent doing all the many tests on the many different pieces of equipment that were required, both on the fire engines themselves and at the fire station.

That is, unless you were the duty cook! Then, your job was to prepare and cook Sunday roast dinner with all the trimmings and a sweet for twelve ravenous firemen. Lunch was served about 1 p.m., calls permitting.

After washing up and cleaning the kitchen, the rest of the shift was on stand-down until the night shift arrived and for some, it was a time to catch up on their sleep after a late Saturday night out on the town.

Although being the duty cook was something new to most recruits, everyone had to do their turn on a Sunday when there was no civilian cook on duty.

The remainder of the crew would help to prepare the vegetables and then would leave you alone to complete the meal. They always wanted a roast dinner in those days, followed by a sweet. Although cooking the vegetables and roasting the meat were not too much of a problem for me, Yorkshire pudding and a sweet were different. The rule was if you served a bad meal, you would be cook the next time and so on until you did get it right. Not knowing how to cook a sweet, I phoned home for some advice, but unfortunately, no one was in.

Thinking to myself that cooking a rice pudding couldn't be too difficult, I measured out one cup of rice for every fireman. I then put the rice into trays in the oven and covered it in milk, keeping a close eye on the rice and adding more and more milk as the rice swelled. Eventually, we ran out of milk and as I did not have enough trays to put the ever swelling rice into, I then added some water.

We ended up with enough rice to feed half of India and it was like concrete! However, I was a quick learner, so my next try was a complete success.

I still love to cook, but still over cater on my portions when cooking at home. Anyway, that's the excuse I use for being overweight now.

One Sunday, when I was not cook, there were no Leading Firemen on duty at the start of the shift and I was told, "You will be Acting Leading Fireman for the day", a common practice when you have passed the examination for the rank.

This would mean that I was to take charge of the first appliance to turn out to a fire that only required one appliance to attend. A single appliance was normally crewed by a team of six men maximum and four men minimum. The day in question was in the middle of summer and due to leave etc, we were at the minimum strength of four men.

After a large lunch, my boss announced that he was going to catch up on some sleep, his last words being, "If you are called out, don't ask for more appliances, or you will get a bollocking from me later, especially if I am disturbed" and off to the dormitory he went.

The alarm sounded about an hour later. One appliance to a grass fire near the woods in a village about a fifteen minute journey away. Quickly getting dressed into our kit, we set off to find the fire, until about five minutes away from reaching the scene, a large plume of black smoke could be clearly seen rising into the sky. No real cause for concern, as field fires were often like that, but I was starting to sweat a little, wondering what was on fire, as it seemed be getting worse by the minute.

Arriving at the site of the fire, we were faced with the problem of access, as the fire was on a hillside about a quarter of a mile away, with no vehicle access.

A very large fire was raging, both in the fields surrounding a large wooded area and the woods themselves were also involved.

Leaving the appliance, I went to investigate the scale of the fire. Normally at this time, an assistance message would be sent to Fire Control, but all I could think about was *"Don't you call me out!"* - the words kept coming back to me. I knew I really needed assistance, but would this prevent my promotion in the future? After all, the fire might put itself out as quickly as it started, as they sometimes did.

In the woods there was a road, more of a track really, but it meant we could get the appliance closer to the seat of the fire. At this point, the wind gusted and it seemed to me that the whole of the woods was on fire. I had one appliance with four men including myself and no water other than the 400 gallons that we carried on board. I had no choice, I had to radio for help. I requested three more appliances and I knew that the Senior Fire Officer would also be sent.

As the Senior Fire Officer approached and saw the column of black smoke, he requested a further two appliances, making six in total.

Many hours later, the fire was out and we returned to the station and with that went straight home as the night watch was already on duty.

I never had a bollocking, but years later I told my boss about it. He laughed and said he never meant what he had said and he didn't believe I had delayed in asking for help.

I never ever delayed an assistance call again!

The Aircraft Crash

Returning to my earlier days. Another weekend and I found myself acting Leading Fireman again. The appliance with the Sub Officer in charge was out at a job and we had just returned from a call to a small grass fire.

Shortly after returning to the station, the bells went down again. In fact, they were not bells at all, but a high pitched alarm. When the alarm sounds, the lights at the fire station all come on and the doors to the appliance bays open automatically.

"One appliance to aircraft crashed into field", says the message from Fire Control

'Bloody hell!', I think to myself, 'A plane crash and I'm on my own!'. As we speed towards the call, lights flashing and sirens sounding, my adrenalin is flowing at record levels.

How do you deal with a plane crash? What if people are trapped? These thoughts, plus many others race through your mind as every minute brings us closer to the scene.

It is right in the middle of the summer and most appliances in the county appear to be out fighting the many grass and undergrowth fires, so we are on our own with no back-up being immediately available.

Then, in the distance, we see the tail plane of a light aeroplane sticking up in the air, with the nose stuck into ground at the side of the road. Also visible are marks across an adjacent ploughed field, where it looked like the pilot had tried to make an emergency landing, only to be beaten by the drainage ditch at the side of the road and into which the nose of the small aeroplane had ended up.

At this time, it did not occur to me, or to the other firemen, what was strange, or out of the ordinary at the scene. Skidding to a halt beside the light aircraft, with its nose in the roadside ditch, we all leap out ready for action and looking for information from the sole policeman in attendance.

The look on his face was one of total amazement. He asked, "What the hell are you doing here?".

"Dealing with this incident?", I replied. Suddenly, I thought to myself, 'Where was everyone else? Why was there only one policeman there and he did not even have his lights flashing?'.

"Well, you're lot are a bit bloody late. It crashed four hours ago. The three people aboard are all right, apart from some bruises to body and ego and they left hours ago."

He was only there waiting for the plane to be recovered.

So, after a quick look around, we returned red faced and feeling slightly stupid back to the fire station, very relieved that we had not had to deal with an aircraft crash, without any assistance.

False Alarms

False alarms make up the largest percentage of the emergency calls received by the Fire Services. However, not all of these are malicious calls and many are via an automatic fire alarm system.

These calls happen on a regular basis for a variety of reasons.

For example, during the summer months, when windows are open, insects find their way into the detectors and then the alarm sounds. Hairsprays, air-fresheners, paint fumes and any number of other things can trigger the detector heads.

These calls are a nuisance to the brigades, but they have to be attended and until you arrive there is no way of knowing if there is a fire or not. The occupiers may be busy making sure that people at their premises are safe before investigating the circumstances. ·

Smoke and fumes from kitchens are another source of calls, setting off nearby detectors.

Sometimes, outside smoke, or burning smells are drawn into buildings by the ventilation system, in the process setting off the alarm. In a large building, the source can be difficult to locate, so fire appliances are tied up trying to find the source, or perhaps it's a real fire.

During the time I was a fireman at my first station, we were regularly called out to the same places time and time again - all false alarms. The County Council, in their wisdom, said that something had to be done about the large numbers of calls across the county that were costing so much money to attend and that in future, regular calls to the same address, for a false alarm caused by an unknown fault on the fire alarm system, would invoke a charge. Perhaps, then the systems would be serviced more regular and cut down the number of false alarms.

This did not last long, because it cost the County Council even more money when it was realised that County Hall and other council-owned premises were one of the worst offenders.

Late one night in 1974, the alarm sounded in the station. Both appliances to respond to an automatic alarm at an old people's home. We had been to this home on many occasions. We were also informed from Fire Control that many calls had been received about this particular fire. This told the crews that this was a serious fire and people were trapped inside.

Approaching, we could see the glow of the fire and pall of smoke rising into the night sky and this told us that this was certainly no false alarm.

One section of the building was engulfed in flames and smoke, with the other parts rapidly filling with deadly smoke and fumes.

The request was quickly made to Fire Control to increase the number of fire appliances needed to assist, both with the fire fighting and rescue of any one still trapped in the building.

Once inside, we explained to the residents that there was a serious fire and they must get up immediately and leave. It was obvious that this was not going to work, as the smoke filled the bedrooms, making it difficult for ourselves to breathe without breathing apparatus.

So, we just rolled them up in their bedding and passed them out of the windows as fast as we could, before they even knew what was happening

The last appliances would not leave until 24 hours later.

So, among others, the biggest lesson learned was never take automatic calls for granted. I will never forget this fire and its very tragic consequences and from then onwards, I always treated all alarms as real, no matter how many times I had been called out previously for nothing.

Many of the old residents were deep in sleep, due to age, some due to drugs to help them sleep and the time of night. Added to this was the fact that many of the residents would have been incapable of self rescue even in normal circumstances.

Eight appliances were called to help and the rescue of people began as soon as the first appliances arrived and continued until it was certain everyone in the building had been accounted for, which was not until hours later.

I remember entering the first smoke-filled bedroom that we came to and gently trying to wake up an old man. Naturally he was both shocked and bewildered at being gently shaken awake by two complete strangers in a dark and smoke-filled room and he just could not take in what was happening. We knew that we had to act fast if we were to get him out and then try to rescue any more people from the blazing building.

Wrapping him up in his bedding, we carried him to the window where we passed him outside onto the ground. Luckily, it was on the ground floor, so he was quickly helped.

We then moved on to the next bedroom, where this time we just grabbed the person and repeated what we had done in the first room, but this time without any explanations as time was of the essence and the smoke thickened by the second.

Our breathing was becoming extremely difficult as we made our way from room to room. Finally, we had to stop because of to the heavy toll hot and smoke filled conditions were having, leaving us retching and gasping for air outside.

All the time, other crews with the benefit of breathing apparatus, continued to search and rescue what residents they could from the inferno.

Tragically, 18 people died in this fire and approximately 10 were rescued by the brigade, with some assistance from at least one police officer who helped me in the early stages of the incident.

Later on, I was taken to hospital, where I was treated for smoke inhalation, before being discharged the next day.

I will never understand why, to my knowledge, no fireman was awarded any sort of commendation for that night's work.

Many firemen and at least one police officer carried out their duties that night with very great degree of bravery and professionalism that helped to rescue 10 people.

Apparently, the then Chief Fire Officer considered that we were only doing what we were paid to do, so should not receive any rewards, not even a letter of thanks.

Many months later, all the fire crews who had attended this tragic event were ordered to go to a civic presentation, where many presentations were handed out to the many people who the county council said were worthy of recognition for their contributions that night and during the following days. The place was dripping with bouquets of flowers and other gifts. No fire service personnel received any awards and many firemen left the presentation before the end, understandingly very disappointed.

Kegworth Church

During periods of extreme weather, you can guarantee the Fire Service will be called out to help someone, somewhere.

In times of extreme heat waves and drought, the Fire Services would be stretched, to use the press's language, as grass fires, undergrowth fires and even forest fires escalated. Sometimes these were natural, but unfortunately many were started accidentally, or even deliberately. The number of calls always escalated during the long school holidays.

Other extremes of weather also increased the number of calls received; high winds blowing down trees onto roads, or at the worst, on to people or vehicles.

Also structural damage to buildings, making them unsafe, again resulting in the Fire Services being called out.

High rainfall, especially over a very short time span, can quickly result in flash flooding in local areas and once again out go the services.

Much time is spent pumping water out of buildings, but sometimes this is just a token gesture, as there is nowhere to pump the water as water levels in these areas are so high that the water flows back as quick as it is pumped away.

It is only when the rain has stopped and the levels subside that pumping is successful.

The only thing is that it gives comfort to the unlucky people caught up in these flash floods.

Usually, Fire Officers have to assess which calls have priority for the pumping appliances and those that put people in danger obviously had priority. A flooded cellar, where the electricity meter was threatened by water, would be more likely to be pumped out before a cellar which had no meters or other dangers in it.

One of these less important calls was to the crypt at Keyworth Church, just outside of Nottingham. So, it was a few days after the downpour that we were sent to the church.

Because the appliance could not access the church yard, we had to use a portable pump, described in the manual as 'easily handled by two men'.

But, what the manual failed to say was only if they were built like Arnie Schwarzenegger in his prime!

Four firemen struggled to carry the pump between the gravestones, before connecting the suction hose to the pump and lowering this hose it into the crypt. The pumps at this time were not fitted with electric starters and had to be cranked with a starting handle. They could be very hard to start at times and this was one of those days.

The fireman took turns on the starting handle, pulling against the compression, until it felt your arms would pull out.

Time passed and there was not a sign of life from the pump. The only sound being that of swear words used to describe the pump!

Suddenly, we were all aware of a presence and there stood the local vicar, who had obviously overheard our very colourful language. "Having trouble, boys?", he said, looking heavenwards and then back to us. The next second, the pump burst into action and although I don't know if the vicar had asked for help, it was very impressive and we all suffered guilt complexes for our bad language in this sacred place. Afterwards, he had a wry smile on his face as he thanked us for our efforts.

Chapter Six

Promotion

With promotion, I was transferred to the busiest station in the new County Fire Brigade - Nottingham Central. The County and City Fire Brigades were separate brigades when I joined the service and in 1974 they had amalgamated into one brigade.

The 'city' firemen thought they were superior to the 'county' fireman, due mainly to the fact that they were very busy and attended more fires.

Some of them also resented having former county men in charge, so it was with some trepidation that I moved to the new station, that is new to me, not a new building.

Talk about being thrown into the deep end!

On my very first day as Leading Fireman, I was to act up to the rank of Sub Officer. The calls came thick and fast and I was soon brought down to earth when an older member of the crew told me, "You might be in charge, but you are still a member of the crew, so get stuck in and get pull your bloody weight!".

I will never forget this and I then started to fit in at my new station. However, to this day, the real old 'city' men still call me a 'county wanker' and all the men transferred into the city from the county, whatever their rank, are still known as 'county men'. This was long ago and no longer happens as everyone who remained commenced after the amalgamation of the two brigades.

Based at a station in the heart of a city, you really did see life, especially when the main police station was next door and shared the station yard, the magistrates' courts backing onto both of us.

We had hundreds of calls during my time there and I really enjoyed it.

The down side was that I also saw more deaths by fire in my relative short time there than some people would see in their entire careers.

One memory of my time was being attacked during the inner city riots of years ago, all fire appliances having to have police protection.

This had never, in my experience, ever happened before The public always used to respect what we did, but sadly things declined from here and nowadays it is more common to be attacked, or have equipment stolen while attending incidents.

My years at Central were both hard and rewarding and I only left for further promotion.

Returning to my promotion at Central, I was eager to show that I was to be a good Leading Fireman on one occasion, a fire in an upstairs store room of a shoe shop left a mess in the upstairs rooms.

While the officer-in-charge was talking to a police officer, I decided to get on with the job and ordered the fire crews to clear out all the debris by throwing it out of the windows into the yard at the back of the premises.

We had just about finished, when I heard the O.I.C. tell the Police officer, "Yes, I suspect arson, so I've left the room so that you can inspect the evidence".

I had to take him to one side and explain what I had done; luckily he could see the funny side and never mentioned it again.

All things in life have a habit of biting if you are not careful and you never ever stop learning, especially from your mistakes.

Promotion came again and I was transferred to Dunkirk, a city station as Sub Officer in charge of Green watch, where I would remain for eighteen years and which were also the best years of my career. I would go to many other stations on secondment and even back to Central as the Station Officer in charge, but Dunkirk was where I was happiest and was determined to stay, only to retire when failing a routine medical with injuries collected over my career.

Some firemen on the shift served me throughout the eighteen years and they remain friends in retirement, as do many others from other stations. However, there must be some who did not like me, that's life!

We worked hard together and we played hard together. We all knew each other's families and shared their ups and downs. If you were ever in trouble with anything, someone would always help, or they would know someone else who could help.

Many of the old city firemen had trades: electrician, joiner, plumber and the like, because the old City Brigade at one time only recruited tradesmen.

If the tradesmen could not help, they knew someone who could, so you were never stuck for anything (within reason!).

One day, I happened to mention that I had tried to obtain tickets to see a show at a Nottingham nightclub, but that they were sold out. "Don't worry, I have a mate who will get you and your wife in", said a colleague. On the day, he phoned to tell me he would meet me in the foyer at 7.00 p.m. and get my wife and me in.

"Tickets, please", asked the doorman.

"Sorry, I'm waiting for a friend who has the tickets", I replied.

"OK, wait over there."

We waited and waited, even asking if the tickets had been left in the foyer.

As I asked, I overheard some other people say they were friends of the band, so they were allowed in, but told no seats were available, so to stand near the bar and wait for their friends in the band.

So, when the person asked, "Can I help, sir?".

I replied, "Friends of the band".

"You know there are no seats, sir. Just stand by the bar."

Much to my wife's embarrassment, we went inside, had a few drinks, watched the show and then went home.

"How embarrassing!", said my wife.

"Well at least you were able to see the show", said my laughing colleague, who had failed to produce the tickets. "Not my fault", he added, "They were supposed to be waiting".

To this day, I think I was set up, but he always maintained the tickets should have been there

Cattle Truck

One sunny afternoon in early spring, I was in charge of an appliance from Central Fire Station, Nottingham *en route* via London Road for the Meadows area, to inspect the local hydrants.

It was one of the first warm spring afternoons after the usual grim winter and one of those days that put a spring in your step and a smile on your face.

Passing our appliance and coming to a stop ahead of us at a red traffic light, was a very expensive sports car, top down, with a male driver and a very good looking young lady in the passenger seat.

With the wind whipping through their hair, the couple were laughing and smiling at each other, oblivious to anything around them.

At the side of the sports car in the nearside lane, was a lorry and our appliance stopped behind the lorry.

Suddenly, out of the side of the lorry, came a stream of dark brown of very liquid cow muck, which cascaded all over the two shocked occupants of the sports car.

With that, the whole crew doubled up with laughter at what appeared to us to be the funniest thing we had ever witnessed.

The moral of the story is, don't park next to a cattle truck in an open top car, especially if the passenger is not your wife, or girlfriend, because then you are in even more s**t!.

Yes, despite the laughter, we did tried to assist them, but neither of them would give names, as it was obvious that both were married, but not to each other and they had just been out for a spot of lunch, but had not planned this for 'afters'.

Dunkrik Fire Station

Dunkirk Fire station had two appliances when I transferred there: a water tender ladder and a water tender and we had twelve personnel per watch, consisting of myself in charge, two leading firemen and nine firemen.

However, this number of firemen would be reduced to seven, when the water tender was taken away to be replaced by a hydraulic platform.

The station area only covered about one square mile, but we still covered up to 3,000 calls per year in my later years, when the hydraulic platform was moved and the rescue tender was transferred to Dunkirk.

This appliance was very busy as it covered about a quarter of the entire county, backing up other appliances at any type of rescue, from RTAs to animal rescues, or people trapped in machinery etc. Some of the crews were keen to man this appliance, but others not so.

The station was backed up by a Fire Prevention Department, which was located in a house at the side of the station yard, which had been built originally by the Nottingham City Brigade to house one of its officers. Later on, this department would move into the main station.

Their staff consisted of a Station Officer, Sub Officer and a civilian administrator.

We had two cooks, one on days and one at night and a cleaner who came in five days a week. Due to cuts in finance, the night cook was phased out, so it was up to the watches what they had for supper. Some always cooked a meal, while other stations never had a cooked meal for everyone at night.

It seemed that most of the busy stations in the south of the county all still had supper, but the stations in the north of the county did not.

This had some effect on us, because when reporting for duty, you were sent out to other stations to cover shortages. These stations were supposed to provide you with a meal, but this was not the case at these northern stations and this sometimes led to ill feeling and hungry firemen.

On duty for Christmas, it was always the old tradition that the officers cooked the Christmas dinner. I worked lots of Christmases and always cooked, or helped to cook the meal.

The tables would be covered by real tablecloths, complete with flowers and serviettes. Soup, roast dinner with all the trimmings, followed by Christmas pudding and custard would be served with a choice of red or white wine, followed by a cigar and brandy, then in the afternoon our families would come into the station for games and laughter, calls permitting.

I must say that the drivers refrained from any drink, but would enjoy another meal with drink when they were not driving at a later shift. We certainly enjoyed our Christmas.

As said earlier, we had two appliances at Dunkirk, so were never as busy as Central, but as each year passed, the busier we became.

Later on, the rescue tender was transferred to Dunkirk and we became even busier, attending RTAs in the entire south of the county.

So, new skills had to be learned and many of the victims of serious accidents owe their lives to the skills of these men.

Over the years, we worked closely with both the police and ambulance services, so that our individual jobs dovetailed into theirs, producing a combined team effort that has helped many people and animals.

The hospital teams were also combined into training together with all the services, so as to further the needs of trapped personnel. I feel very proud to have been a small part of this development, but am saddened that on retirement through whatever means, age or injury etc, that this vital knowledge and training is suddenly thrown onto the scrap heap.

How many times have I watched the news of a disaster somewhere, knowing that a great many people with a mass of knowledge and expertise, such as myself, were just forced to have to watch on television, when they would in some way like to have been able to assist.

In writing this book, I have put together some of my recollections that I think are worthy of a mention, but these are only a tiny part of thirty-one great years serving the people of Nottingham.

All of the calls received over the years were treated seriously; many were tragic and many were routine, while many were false alarms of various types.

But, every incident attended usually involved the fireman's never-ending sense of humour, mostly black and only understood by those who served. These were the days when firemen wanted to be firemen because they were proud of the job

Steam on the Met as N2 No. 69523 heads for Harrow on the Hill.

Myself on No. 69523 awaiting departure from Neasden sidings.

Driving No. 61264, heading towards Amersham with a packed train before the engine was stopped the following day with leaking seams in the firebox.

Steam to spare as we pace the electric underground train so photographers can take action photos.

No. 35005 *Canadian Pacific* leaves Ropley for Alton.

Neasden underground shed in the background as No. 61264 approaches the old Neasden steam shed for servicing.

Merchant Navy Class No. 35005 *Canadian Pacific* awaits departure as
West Country Class 34105 *Swanage* approaches
Meadstead & Four Marks station.

Castle Class No. 7029 *Clun Castle* stands in the platform at Loughborough.

Class A2 No. 60532 *Blue Peter* stand in the evening sun outside Loughborough engine shed.

A Midland day as Class 4 No. 44422, Class 8 No. 48305 and Jubilee Class No. 45596 *Bahamas* are prepared for the day's work

No. 35005 *Canadian Pacific* stands at Carlisle Upperby shed after working over the Settle to Carlisle line.

After servicing the locomotive, the support crew have their photograph taken in front of No. 35005 *Canadian Pacific* at Chester. The owner of No. 35005 at the time - Andrew Naish - is third from the left , the author second from the right.

Coronation Class No. 46229 *Duchess of Hamilton* powers along the
Great Central Railway.

No. 4472 *Flying Scotsman* and *Blue Peter* stand outside Loughborough shed.

No. 61264 at speed as it revisits its old territory in East Anglia.

Hall Class No. 6990 *Witherslack Hall* races south in the sun and snow.
(Photographer unknown)

West Country Class Nos. 34039 *Boscastle*, 34101 *Hartland* and Merchant Navy Class No. 35005 *Canadian Pacific* are prepared for their next workings.

Barrow Hill shed and No. 61264 poses as No. 61039 *Steinbok* for a photographic charter.

Another view as No. 61039.

No. 61039 leaves Barrow Hill sidings with a northbound fitted freight.

No. 61264 Passes near to Toton East on a charter from London.

No. 61264 prepares to leave Grosmont with a pick-up goods.

No. 61264 backs into Grosmont after arriving from York.

In the sidings at Grosmont.

On the East Coast Main Line, No. 61264 leaves Peterborough in the dark, bound for King's Cross.

Jubilee Class *Kolhapur* and No. 61039 in the roundhouse at Barrow Hill.

No. 61264 leaving Norwich in 2006.

Leaving Mallaig for Fort William on the steam service.

they did and when counselling was not part of our makeup, other than deep discussions back at the station, all served with a large dose of black humour.

Strange, but it was unheard of to be off duty with stress in my earlier career and this 'disorder' only became part of life when we all had to become politically correct, plus the previous standards of entry into the service were made easier.

That will be my last moan, because I really enjoyed my time as a fireman (they say you only remember the good times!).

Talking of good times, what about the bad? So far, I have not mentioned the fireman's strike of 1977.

At this period, firemen did the job because that's what they wanted to do, as while the pay was rubbish, the satisfaction of a job well done out-weighed the monetary rewards. It was why so many firemen found employment when off duty to supplement their poor pay, plus many firemen were time served tradesmen. But, things had to change.

Talk had gone on for ages, with nobody really expecting to strike, although I had seen grown men in tears at the union meetings when the vote for strike action was reluctantly taken.

Certainly, no one thought that we would be on the streets for 10 weeks before the dispute was finally called off.

We went on picket duty as and when we should have been on duty and it was a grim time, what with the weather and no pay.

Sitting with our self-made shelters and braziers that burned for all the 10 weeks, we were later able to shelter in a caravan kindly donated to the cause.

The general public were magnificent to our cause and we were never without some company. Motorists who sounded their horns in sympathy and those who stopped to donate fuel for the braziers, or food and drinks and even money to put into our strike fund.

Even through the long winter's night, people would come to talk and listen and offer all sorts of help.

Some firemen chose not to strike, especially in Nottinghamshire.

This is one of the really bad things, as tempers became frayed and lifetime friendships ended, the repercussions lasting for years afterwards.

For the striking firemen, a lifetime bond would be the result of a very difficult and emotional time for all firemen and their families.

On the positive side, the outcome was a good wage and excellent working conditions, although even that has now disappeared as the most recent fireman's strike did not have the public support of 1977, the fire-fighters losing many of their good conditions.

A story during the strike: it was a Sunday afternoon and I had gone for a walk with my dog (not the wife, a four-legged one!)

It was bitterly cold as I arrived home, when my wife informed me she had called 999 to report the house across the road on fire.

We knew that this particular house was empty, so we settled back to watch the Army with their Green Goddess and the Air Force with their Land Rover deal with the incident.

Anyway, they soon had the fire out and I settled down with a cup of tea to watch TV.

Answering a knock at the door, my wife found an Army man asking if she would make tea for the crew, as the Green Goddess had broken down and they were fire fighting for the public.

"I will ask my husband first", she said, "As he is on strike from the Fire Brigade".

"Oh! I'm so sorry", he said, "Of all the houses to ask! I'll ask someone else".

I heard the conversation and invited them in for tea and although they declined to come in, we did give them tea and they were most embarrassed.

However, they were only doing what they were ordered to do and I had no problem with that.

Another incident which occurred while I was on picket duty was that one evening just before Christmas, I was sat alongside the brazier and next to the large Christmas tree that some kind person had donated to the cause.

There was a strange silence!

All of a sudden, I was surrounded by the local vicar and his band of choristers. Wishing me and all the striking firemen a Merry Christmas, they asked if I would like to select a couple of carols and it was then I realised that there were no other firemen around.

Where had they suddenly disappeared too?

I heard later, that my mates, who had spotted the arrival of the carol singers, decided to go and hide, leaving me to face them and make a donation to parish funds. Also, they thought it would be very funny if I was left to face them alone.

Looking towards the fire station, I saw them all hiding around the corner, leaving me, the least religious of anyone, to face the carol singers and vicar.

I did manage to name a couple of carols, but suggested to the vicar, rather than me choose an appropriate prayer, that he choose one for me.

Finally, they wished me well and went on their way around the parish, leaving me on my own.

To be fair, I did offer to make a small donation, but the vicar suggested they should be making a donation to our fund.

Bless you vicar and your flock.

One Long Night

Night shift at Dunkirk Fire Station was from 18.00 hrs until 09.00hrs the next morning - 15-hours. A long shift, which always started off by checking over all the equipment carried on the appliances and your own personal kit. This was usually followed by practical, or theoretical training until 21.00 hrs when supper would be taken, cooked by our regular night cook.

After supper, the crews were allowed to relax, or study at their own pace for any promotion exams.

Later, they would be able to rest on their beds until 07.00 hrs, when they then worked on various tasks until relieved at 09.00 hrs.

Emergency calls could come at any time and would be responded to as required. My station was a City station and it was very rare not to be called out at sometime, especially during a night shift.

The night in question had not long begun. Just after all the equipment had been checked, the sound of tortured metal was heard on the ring road adjoining the fire station, to be quickly followed by the station alarm.

It was a road traffic accident on the ring road outside the station. Less than a hundred yards outside the station, a car was upside down on top of the crash barrier on the nearside of the road, the driver being trapped inside, but no other vehicle involved. Being so close, we were the first of the services to arrive, which was quite unusual. Soon afterwards, we were joined by the police and ambulance services and we quickly released the casualty and helped to load him into the ambulance. Despite the combined efforts of the services and with no apparent injuries, the man was declared a fatality at the scene.

The crew had just started to make up the equipment when Fire Control asked if we were available to take another call and we quickly responded to a call reporting a house fire with persons reported. This means people possibly trapped and results in Fire Control dispatching an extra appliance to the normal attendance. The house was on an estate, about one and a half miles away and on approaching the estate, the tell-tale pall of black smoke indicated that this could be serious.

On arrival, a serious fire enveloped the first floor of the house, with the flames spreading into the roofs of the adjoining two houses. The police were already in attendance and informed us that a child was missing in the house. They had been unable to gain entry due to the severity of the fire.

We were joined by two other appliances from a neighbouring station and despite all our efforts, the child sadly perished and the house was severely damaged, plus damage to both the houses on either side. With so much equipment used, we were going to be there for some time, as were the other two appliances from the neighbouring station.

Then, on the radio, Fire Control could be heard dispatching appliances to reports of a large factory on fire, just across the road from our fire station. It was obviously a large fire, as the first appliance in attendance requested more appliances to attend. The two appliances with us were soon sent on to the factory and we remained at the scene until the police had finished their work making sure that everything was recorded for the coroner and that the fire was completely extinguished in all three properties. Fire Control then instructed us to proceed to the neighbouring station to stand-by to provide fire cover for their station area, although to be honest, we all felt disappointed not to be sent to the large factory fire in our own backyard.

When a large fire happens, all firemen want to attend, but we were sent to standby at another station.

This happens when the appliances from a station are tied up at an incident for a long time, cover of station areas being maintained by moving appliances around.

Before we even arrived at this station, we were sent to another call in a residential home, where the automatic fire alarm was sounding.

When we arrived, we found that this alarm was caused by a fault on the alarm system, so our services were not required.

The next call from Control redirected us to another different station to provide cover. We also wanted fresh supplies of compressed air cylinders for our breathing apparatus and oxygen for our resuscitator and so we were made our way to the Central station in the City centre.

While in the process of replenishment of our breathing apparatus cylinders and oxygen cylinders for the resuscitator, the station alarm sounded and we were sent to a report of a fire on an island on the River Trent, possibly with children trapped, near to the border with Derbyshire, about six miles away.

On arrival at the riverbank, we met up with an appliance from Derbyshire and could see a quite large building on fire on an island in the middle of the River Trent. There was no way from our location that we could get to the fire, so leaving the Derbyshire appliance to try to get some water onto the island using a large jet from the riverbank (impossible, but at least something was being tried), we set off to try to obtain a suitable boat from a marina about one mile away.

A request had been made to Fire Control to contact the police to try obtain a suitable vessel and as we arrived, the police already had this in hand. So, loading up with a portable fire pump, hoses and other equipment and after a crash course in how to operate the boat, we prepared to set off upstream, just as the light was fading. At this point, a local woman who was a trained nurse offered to come with us to help with possible casualties.

So, with five firemen, one nurse and all our equipment, we set out for the one-mile journey upstream, with the heavily laden boat sitting very low in the water.

During the journey, the suction hose was connected, the portable pump started and suddenly we had turned into a fireboat. When we arrived at the island, we were quickly able to put out what very little remained of the wooden building and then conduct a search for the children. Shortly afterwards, the Derbyshire appliance on the mainland informed us the children were all safe and well.

It turned out that as an adventure, they had planned to be on the island for the night and they had left a fire burning when they returned to the mainland for some food. When they returned to the bankside, the building had accidentally caught fire (that was their story and they were sticking to it).

Eventually, at about midnight, we made our way back to the marina in the dark to return our equipment, the nurse and, of course, the boat to the anxious owner, who had taken to drink in the boat club bar, worrying if he would ever see his boat again.

Now it was time to return to our station to clean and restock our equipment and have some much-needed refreshments.

Returning to the station, we passed the very large factory fire that was still burning and where many appliances were in attendance. No sooner had we arrived at the station, than we were ordered to go to this factory fire to relieve crews, so that they might have some rest and refreshments.

A rather angry call to Fire Control informed them that our crew had not taken any refreshments and needed to restock with hoses etc. Anyway, apologies soon followed and we were allowed to refresh.

We then attended the factory until about 06.00 hrs, when we were relieved by another crew and sent back to our nearby station. The kettle had not even boiled before the alarms sounded and we were off again to a house fire on the same estate as the earlier tragedy. This again proved to be a serious fire and tied us up to the end of our shift. We were relieved by the day shift at the scene, then made our way wearily back to the station to clean up, before going home some sixteen hours after we had started our night shift.

What a night and the fire reports still had to be completed! I will never forget that night and neither will my crew. We still talk about 'That One Long Night' whenever we get together for a drink or two.

Over the years, there were many busy night shifts, but never one in my career that covered the whole shift with so many and different incidents.

Nottingham's Sewer Systems

Nottingham's sewage system, built in Victorian times, runs under the city streets. In Radford, a very deep sewer runs deep under Ilkeston Road, going up towards Canning Circus, then on to the City Centre and finishes up at Stoke Bardolph a few miles outside the city, near the River Trent.

The engineers at the City Council have the task of maintaining all the sewers under the city and because they were all built a long time ago, unfortunately some of the records have been lost over the years.

In the sewer under Ilkeston Road, the engineers thought that there was an entrance that somehow had become lost and it needed to be found to assist with maintenance of the sewer.

This sewer is about 50-feet under the road and access is via a manhole and then down a system of vertical ladders, leading to the actual sewer itself, which is, perhaps, 10-12-feet in diameter, built of blue engineering bricks and in brilliant condition despite its age. During normal levels, the water and waste flows at a very fast rate towards the city.

The first I knew about this was when we were asked to join a meeting with the City Engineers, where they explained that they were trying to locate this hidden entrance.

This part of the sewer ran through our station area and so we were asked to assist regarding the safety of this operation. Fine, but what was the plan?

The idea was to launch an inflatable boat along the sewer, with city engineers on board the boat with their equipment, including breathing apparatus escape sets and sewer gas detection kits.

The boat would be launched and carried on the current, all the time held on a very long safety line by other personnel in the base of the manhole, which was a large area at the bottom of the manhole

When the crew signalled they had found the old entrance, or the boat reached the end of the line, the idea was the line would be hauled in and the boat and crew retrieved, the length of the line having been deemed long enough by previous calculations.

If there were any problems, a second boat would be launched containing a team of firemen to rescue the first boat!

During the launch of the first boat, the second inflatable boat would be secured to the roof of the sewer and, if necessary, then into the stream.

Again, the second boat would be attached to a long line, so that the boat and crew could be retrieved.

Anyway, that was the plan and we were invited to inspect the site.

It was accessed by vertical ladders, to a depth of about 40-50ft below street level, a long way, especially if wearing full fire kit and breathing apparatus. If sewer gas was present, breathing apparatus would be a necessity. The climb down alone would have a large demand on the contents of the air cylinder, leaving very little time to effect any rescue if gas was present in the entrance and then climb back to the entrance.

This was explained to the engineers, because they had already undertaken some survey work and no sewer gas disturbed, so they agreed to take the risks using small escape breathing sets.

The thing that all the firemen noticed was the distinct lack of foul smells. Yes, there was a smell, but it wasn't too bad.

The speed of the current was quite a surprise seeing that the level was fairly low, but could increase dramatically after a rainstorm, so a weather forecast beforehand was a necessity.

What would happen if the line or rope snapped? Highly unlikely, due to its strength.

In this unlikely event, the boat would be stopped at the next manhole, but this was along way from the starting point and even deeper under the road than from where we started. Fail to stop the boat here and it would be swept onto the city centre and if it was not stopped there, it would be swept on to the sewerage depot at Stoke Bardolph

Not the best plan in the world, with too many unknown problems and not the best solutions to the known problems, but the guinea pig engineers were still keen to give it a try, despite our fears that we may not be able to rescue them.

A short trial was then proposed to test the plan; it would be conducted at night, when both the traffic on the road and passage of water/effluent would be at its lowest.

The teams were assembled at the bottom of the manhole, the crew of three men sat in the boat, with everyone in place both here and at the next manhole and the line was slowly paid out.

The current placed quite a strain on the rope as the boat disappeared down the sewer, the voices of the crew slowly fading away as the rope slowly paid out.

The only communication now a series of horn blasts.

It was quickly realised that the strength of the current would soon sap the strength of the men paying out the rope and the boat then had to be hauled back against the current.

With the firemen now helping, the crew were signalled that they were to be hauled back, but this proved to be very difficult task.

The main reason being that the current had taken the rope downstream faster than the boat had travelled. So, in front of the boat was a large bight of rope, which was collecting any of the nasty things that go down a sewer and forming a very large mass.

This had to be pulled against the current and past the boat, before we could start to retrieve the boat itself. A very hard and unpleasant job, but finally the boat and crew were back at the bottom of the manhole, much to the relief of us all.

With everyone safely back at street level, it was decided the test was not a success and the plan was abandoned.

A very relieved set of firemen returned to their stations for a shower and well earned meal. Our thoughts with the men who work the sewers every day of their working lives and they deserve all the money they earn. How many of us ever think about the people who do these dirty smelly jobs, just to make our lives better? I often wondered if they ever located the lost entrance.

Thinking of sewers reminds me of a true story at our fire station. Dunkirk had always suffered from problems with the drains and sewers, but nothing seemed to be done about it.

I had a bee in my bonnet about this, so was always trying to get the problem solved, not realising how much the firemen were getting bored with the subject.

One morning, nearly at the end of our night shift, I went as usual into the toilets before washing and shaving ready to parade off duty.

As I entered the toilet, I could not believe my eyes, the biggest turd I had ever seen, curled around the toilet pan and even protruded upwards near to the seat.

No wonder we had problems with the sewers, but more importantly, what had this monster done to someone's backside.

Using the station Tannoy, I called all personnel to report immediately to the toilets.

"Who's responsible for this?", I asked.

No one owned up, but Pete Sisson - one of the firemen - said, "Don't worry, I'll sort it". He then plunged his hand down the toilet bowl, attempting to clear it out, but as it broke up and covered his hand and arm in s**t, I called out, "You dirty sod!" and with that, I had to leave the toilets before I was sick.

While sitting in the office looking and feeling ill, I was aware that all the watch members had great big grins on their faces. At this point I knew I had been had.

Pete Sisson had spent two days making a plaster of Paris imitation turd, even painting it!

During his time making it at his home, his mother-in-law had asked him what on earth was he making and when he replied a giant turd, she never even blinked, or even asked why.

Incidentally, shortly afterwards, we had a camera survey of our drains and sewers before the problem was finally fixed

Accident & Emergency

One morning, I answered the office telephone and found myself talking to the Accident & Emergency department of the nearby hospital. They had a delicate problem. A patient was in their department and he had his testicles trapped in a chair. Would we send a crew to try and release him? The mind ran wild with painful thoughts for this poor man and how and why he was trapped. Alerting both the crew of our fire appliance and the crew of the rescue tender, I made a radio call to Fire Control, who knew nothing of our mission. 'Both appliances mobile to the hospital to man with trapped testicles' was possibly the only time this radio message had ever been sent. Control thought they must be hearing things, as they asked for confirmation of our message.

On our arrival, we were led into the operating theatre, where on the operating table was our patient, lying on his side with a white plastic chair attached to him by his testicles, which by this had swollen to double their normal size.

The doctors and nurses had tried their best, but had been unable to help the poor man.

The fact that he was elderly and had a serious heart condition added to the problem. Cut the chair so that we were only dealing with the seat part was to be our first action; this was a slow process as any movement caused severe pain to the patient. The crew were wet through during this process, because we were wearing full fire kit and sweating, both with the heat of the operating theatre and the tension of the situation.

Despite his pain and embarrassment, the old boy managed to retain some humour during his ordeal, as we constantly promised that we would rescue him and save his wedding tackle.

After reducing the chair to a manageable size, we were still faced with the problem of how to release him intact. Due to the swelling and type of seat, we were unable to use any normal type of saw, or cutting device. All methods were tried and rejected before we came up with the answer. Luckily, both for the patient and ourselves, the rescue tender carried a cutting wire that had only been issued a few days before this call.

Basically, it was like a cheese wire, but was coated with abrasives that allowed even metal to be cut. The wire was carefully fed through the same aperture as the testicles and cuts were made working away from the delicate area, while holding the chair seat rigid to prevent movement and pain. All this time, we had to cool the cutting wire by spraying water onto the cutting area from a large syringe. After a number of cuts, the patient was finally released, with nothing more than having to wait for the swelling to go down and the embarrassment to fade away.

How did he come to be in this predicament you ask? Well he was having a bath, but was unable to get into or out of the bath on his own. Nursing staff had lifted him into the bath by a hoist. Lifting him out by hoist, he was placed onto a plastic chair, so they could dry him off. Unfortunately, as they lowered him into the chair, his weight forced his testicles through the small holes in the base of the chair and efforts to move him caused them to quickly swell up, so trapping him and increasing the swelling.

Luckily only his pride was permanently injured!

Throughout this long operation, a member of the hospital operating team had been taking Polaroid photographs of the event, to be used as a training aid and to have a permanent record for the future. With the permission of the patient, I asked if it was possible to have a copy of them for the same reasons. A few days later, I received a set of the photos, complete with an invoice for the cost of them from the good old National Health Service.

I sent the bill back with an invoice of my own; for the cost of two fire appliances plus the fee for seven firemen and asked them to take off the cost of the photographs from my bill.

The next day, a rather embarrassed lady telephoned to apologise and sensibly both bills were torn up.

Many times our appliances been called to the Accident & Emergency Department to remove all sorts of items from various parts of the anatomy, both male and female, where the embarrassment of the patients usually means they do not experiment again so quickly. Children though are always getting things stuck, so we were called out quite regularly.

A lot of these calls were after sessions of a sexual nature, calling for a steady hand, but one call we had was to a local pub, where a woman was reported stuck.

We arrived to find a very embarrassed lady, glued to the telephone handset. The handset was glued to her ear and hand after someone thought it would be funny to leave superglue on the handset of a public phone.

However, this was an easy job; just cut the cable and send her to hospital to have the handset removed.

To save her further embarrassment, we wrapped a towel round her head like a headscarf and left her sitting in casualty awaiting her turn.

Talking of ladies, how not to rescue people, or how not to treat them after rescuing them.

It was shortly after lunchtime and we had been called to a flat fire in a multi-storey block of flats at Lenton.

The message said 'flat fire with persons reported'.

This told us that persons were most probably involved in the fire and ensured that an extra appliance would be dispatched to assist.

Arriving at the tower block, smoke was to be seen from a window about ten floors up. So, taking the internal staircase, we made our way to the scene.

The corridors were filled with thick, black evil smoke and our team of breathing apparatus wearers were sent in to search for the woman reported inside.

Shortly afterwards, the team located the woman and brought her out onto the staircase, not too badly affected by the smoke. The breathing apparatus team then returned to the fire fighting.

Meanwhile the woman explained that she did not live there and was married to someone else, so really needed to be gone.

I was sympathetic and agreed after making sure she was fine, but then she asked if she could retrieve her handbag, just as the team said they had the fire under control.

She explained that her bag was just inside the door, so I let her into the building to retrieve it.

Within seconds, there was a flashover and we had to return to the safety of the staircase.

The breathing apparatus team were uninjured and soon dealt with the fire and were able to rescue the woman - for the second time within 15 minutes.

This time she needed oxygen and treatment from the paramedics, but refused hospital treatment.

I had the Mickey taken out of me for allowing the woman back inside and the moral is don't let your heart rule when there are dangerous circumstances. I was very lucky the woman was not seriously hurt, or killed - another valuable lesson.

The Goldfish

During my years as a fire officer, I attended many strange calls, but one of the strangest incidents actually came direct to the fire station. It was evening and we were on the night shift, having just finished a training session, when the phone rang and Fire Control asked for me on the telephone.

"This is not a joke", emphasised the control room operator, "A woman is on her way to the fire station and is bringing with her a pet goldfish which is trapped, inside a plastic boot at the bottom of its bowl". The operator added that the RSPCA had been out to the woman's house, but had been unable to release the goldfish, so the Fire Brigade had been called as the last resort.

At the time, I must admit that I did look at the calendar, just to make sure it was not a joke on April 1st!

The woman eventually arrived in the company of an RSPCA officer and placed the goldfish bowl, complete with the trapped fish on my desk.

In the bottom of the bowl was a plastic boot, the type usually used by a small gerbil, or hamster to play in. The fish had obviously swam into a hole in the side of the boot and tried to swim through the boot and come out the other side, something it had done on many other occasions. Unfortunately, this time it became stuck halfway out of the boot, but why this had happened, we would never know.

The bowl was much too small for the firemen to get their hands into, so we had to transfer the boot and fish into a large bucket of water. At this stage, the woman said, "If anything happens to him, I will sue you all

"Thanks madam", I replied.

With the aid of a junior hacksaw blade, we made a couple of cuts each side of the boot, protecting the fish from the blade by inserting feeler gauges between the fish and boot, then with a little gentle persuasion, the boot was slightly opened out and the fish was free. Sounds straightforward, but under water in a bucket, it was a delicate little operation that took a fair time to complete

A good result, even if the expression on the face of goldfish did not change when rescued, but both fish and owner went away very happy. After much laughter and joking, we retired for the night. Shortly after midnight, the telephone began to ring. It was the newsroom of a London daily paper who wanted the story of the rescued goldfish and could they send a reporter and photographer to the station?

"Not until after 07.00 hrs the next morning", I told them.

Just after 07.00 hrs, a Porsche car arrived in the station yard, driven by an independent photographer, accompanied by the woman, complete with her hair done and make up on and yes, the goldfish bowl and fish.

The photographs were duly taken, using a fish-eye lens on the camera (honestly!) with the smiling woman holding what she said was 'a happy fish' and was taken away to live their moment of fame. I understand that the photographer made quite a bit of money when his pictures sold around the world.

When we went off shift at 09.00 hrs the following day, the phone was still ringing, newspaper editors everywhere wanting pictures and the story. The calls continued to my home all through the next day from all over the world, wanting details of the story.

Eventually getting fed up with the calls, I asked, "Why the interest?".

They replied, "When did you last hear of a trapped goldfish being released by seven fireman?".

I had to admit never!

So, this incident rated higher than many more serious incidents that hardly made the local news, never mind the nationals or the world's press. Makes you wonder what a strange world we live in.

Terrier in the Cliffs

Animals seem to get themselves frequently into situations that call for help to release them. Everyone asks about the cat stuck up a tree, but usually, if left long enough, hunger finally forces them down.

So, our policy was not to risk the lives of firemen to rescue animals and if called out by the animal charities, such as the RSPCA, we would attend, but the rescue of the animal, bird etc would be have made by officials of the charity, but with, of course, our help and equipment.

However, the RSPCA was not always available and so we were sometimes sent out to see if we could help.

One such call I remember was by the owners of a Patterdale terrier that had disappeared down a hole and not come back out. The dog had been down the hole for over 24-hrs when we were called, so the owners were pretty distraught by now. Along with friends, they had spent the night digging away to try to locate their dog, unsuccessfully as it turned out, as the hole went behind rock cliffs on the banks of the River Trent just out side of the City.

Making sure it was safe, we listened and called out the dog's name, of which I now cannot remember. Sure enough, we could faintly hear a slight whimper from somewhere behind the rock face. The rock faces being about 30-feet above a public footpath beside the river, when trying to work out where to dig a hole, I noticed that the rock had many cracks running through them, some quite large. The idea then came to me.

If we inserted an airbag into the crack nearest to where we estimated the dog to be, we could then inflate it and hopefully, force the rock away from the cliff without digging. After setting up the equipment and guarding the footpath below, we slowly inflated the bags. Suddenly, about two to three tons of rock was forced away from the cliff face and fell 30-foot onto the path below.

To be honest, we did not know at this point if the dog had gone with it. After a quick check that revealed nothing except rock, we went back onto the cliff face.

More of the hole was now exposed, but still no sound was heard from the dog. Fearing for the dog, we now carefully examined the hole for any sign that would indicate that the animal was still alive.

Suddenly, as my arm entered the hole, I felt the rough fur of the terrier. Feeling its shape, I grasped the skin behind its head and gently prized him from the hole.

Aware that he might be a little tetchy after his ordeal and might be inclined to bite, I quickly passed him to a colleague, who placed him safely onto the ground. He was completely covered in dust, but after shaking himself, he proceeded to do what dogs always do on footpaths. He then sniffed around as though it was quite normal to be trapped for something like 26-hours without food or water.

Later on, I learned that this same dog had been rescued by the Brigade when trapped inside a fallen tree trunk and not far from the scene of its latest escapade.

Another dog rescue featured a St. Bernard puppy. This dog, although only a puppy, was already the size of a Shetland pony.

We received the call from anxious owners that a puppy dog was trapped in a car. Like a lot of calls, there was no other information and when we arrived, we found a very distressed dog and owners. The male owner had arrived home in his car and stopped outside his garage. The puppy, recognising one of its owners, put its front paws onto the windscreen of the car. Its paws then slipped down the windscreen and its paws became trapped between the top of the bonnet in the space where the windscreen wipers are. The more it tried to get out, the more distressed both puppy and owners became. The gloved hands of a couple of firemen applied just enough pressure onto the bonnet, and the paws were gently slid out.

Another successful rescue, although the calming down of both puppy and owners took longer than the rescue. This dog really should have had the brandy barrel round its neck, but not a drop was to be had!

A story that involved another watch at my fire station was funny, although embarrassing for both firemen and the people involved. They received a call to a house where the owners thought that a cat was trapped behind a wall. This young couple had just purchased the house and were preparing to move into it, their very first home.

As they worked away, cleaning throughout the house, they heard a noise that they thought was a sound of a cat from inside one of their walls. Unable to locate the exact location of the cat, they made a call to the RSPCA who, due to other work, were unable to attend, so they asked the Fire Service for help. A fire appliance was sent and the search for the cat started, the couple showing the officers where it was last heard. Sure enough they could hear something, but were unable to pinpoint it. The noise seemed to move around and it would seem that the cat was trapped, or stuck behind a brick wall upstairs.

It was explained to the young couple that we would have to make a hole through the brickwork to try to locate this the animal.

A few swings of the large sledgehammer soon had a hole large enough for a fireman to get his head through to look for the cat. Calling for a torch, a fireman went downstairs to the appliance to get one. On his way back into the building, he was sure he could hear the same sound. As he handed over the torch upstairs, he told the officer-in-charge about the sound.

"Let's check this out", he said, as a fireman declared that there was no cat behind the brickwork upstairs.

Leaving the rubble upstairs, the crew made their way back downstairs and lo and behold, they heard the same noise. One of the firemen then quietly asked the officer-in-charge to accompany him outside.

Once they were outside, he said, "Look what I have just found in a cupboard, sir". Holding up a box, the officer-in-charge saw a smoke alarm. Then it made a noise, the 'purr' an indication that the battery required replacing. *They had found the cat!*

A very embarrassed crew made their way back to the station, leaving an even more embarrassed couple in their new house, complete with new hole in the wall.

Children are always investigating any sort of hole, or space and so occasionally get stuck, or part of them gets stuck. Sometimes they can be freed easily and sometimes it is necessary to get some help.

I never came across anyone with a saucepan on their head, but have helped to free many a child from all sorts of metal objects, many at the local Accident & Emergency unit. So many children turned up over the years, that this department now has a trolley fitted with a vice, so as to hold the object still while it is cut away.

Twice during my career I was involved with rescuing children, who had frozen with fear while climbing down a rock face.

The first was a call to a child trapped on the face of a quarry. He had started to climb down, then when about halfway he froze, too frightened to climb back up, or continue to the bottom. It was a quick job to be lowered down to the boy and then down to the bottom of the quarry. Then we gave him a ride home in the fire engine.

The second time was on the rocks that formed the great hole where Nottingham Victoria Railway station used to be, now the Victoria Shopping complex.

Once again, it was a climb that started out all right for two boys on their way home from school, until about halfway down their courage vanished and all they could do was cry out for help.

Using ropes to climb down to them, we then completed the descent to the bottom of the cutting. From there they were able to walk out via the Victoria Centre car park, back to Huntington Street where they had left their school bags. We gave them a lecture about their stupid behaviour and the danger that they had placed themselves and others, before they were left to make their way home. I always wonder if they ever told their parents.

One day I had been sent as the officer-in-charge at Beeston Fire Station.

Unknown to me, an exercise had been pre-planned for this day, taking place at Toton sidings, where I had worked on the railways.

The scenario was a diesel 2-coach DMU which had crashed into a freight train, which had a Class 37 Diesel at its head.

There were injured passengers in the railcars and the driver was also injured, with the driver of the Class 37 Diesel unconscious in his cab.

All the casualties had labels on them listing their injuries.

Many rail personnel were in attendance and we were informed that due to the nature of the load of the freight train, it contained a threat to trapped passengers and rescuers. It needed to be moved down the sidings to be made safe, but they did not know how long they would have to wait for a driver.

There was complete shock from the organisers as I started up the Class 37 and moved it down the sidings to a safe place.

They had not for one minute expected that a former Toton man would be in charge of the fire crews and would solve the problem so easily. We had quite a laugh about it later when I explained how fate brought me to Toton on this day and not the regular officer who new nothing about starting, uncoupling and then moving a diesel locomotive about the sidings.

Chapter Seven

Back to the Footplate

Once steam has been in the blood, it never leaves it just hibernates, waiting for the chance to course through your veins again.

I was always interested in the railways in general, even after moving on and joining the Fire Service.

One day, after seeing an advertisement for ex-British Railways footplate crew required to help run a heritage railway, I picked up the telephone and volunteered my services at the Midland Railway Centre at Butterley, Derbyshire.

Following an interview, medical and short refresher, including their rules and regulations, I was a steam engine fireman once again.

It really is a small world, as the inspector there was Don Tennant, one of my old drivers at Toton and who was now an inspector at Toton (sadly, no longer with us).

My first turn was as fireman on Stanier Black 5 No. 44932 and it was like I had never been away, the only difference being that coaches were being hauled and not the loose-coupled coal wagons I was used to.

I remember it was 5 a.m., a cold, dark and very windy early start to the day when I arrived at Butterley engine shed. After examining the engine, it was time to break up some pallets to light up the fire. After lighting up, top the tender up with water and then go round and oil up the engine and tender. This was really the driver's job, but having nothing much else to do, I did it while waiting for him.

The driver arrived as the first rays of daylight appeared, proceeding to examine the engine, while I made our first drink of tea. Afterwards, I gave the engine a wipe over to make it look good for the day.

Leaving the shed in good time, we made our way to Butterley station, a short way down the line.

Here, we backed onto the stock and coupled up, connecting the steam heating pipe so as to warm up the coaches and wait until the first departure.

On learning the story of my return to steam, the *Nottingham Evening Post* sent a reporter and photographer to cover the event, which was very good publicity for the railway.

After the last trip of the day, it was back to the shed to put the engine to bed. This involved cleaning the fire, emptying the ash pans and smokebox, before stabling the engine back inside the shed. A quick wash, change out of my overalls and home. It has been a 12-hour day at the railway, without the journey to and from the depot and all for the love of steam. No wonder some people think we must be mad!

I continued to do the occasional shifts at Butterley, mainly on the midweek turns when they were short of crews. I even met some old Toton drivers who also helped out.

Midweek trains at Butterley only ran during the school half-term and summer holidays, so many times when I had days off work, they could not find me work.

The Great Central Railway at Loughborough ran trains everyday through the summer and more during the winter, so here was a chance to help them.

Joining as a member, I was soon set to work in the shed, cleaning out the pits of ash and clinker and also helping with jobs in the shed, maintaining and repairing the fleet of steam locomotives.

I really enjoyed working in the shed, as despite my knowledge, you still started at the bottom and I had never before been involved with this kind of work.

The work could vary from scraping muck, grease and oil off various parts, to filing, cutting with a blow torch, lifting and pulling all sorts of large metal objects and working on a lathe.

It was all new to me, the only familiarity being that you finished the day filthy and some times knackered (in fact, mostly knackered!).

After working in the shed on maintenance and cleaning the engines, I was finally passed out as a fireman. Later on, after a day's written examination and a practical examination, I was passed out as a driver.

During my time as a fireman, I was selected to be a fireman on one of the Great Central engines that was sent to London to work on the London Metropolitan lines of the underground, with a weekend of steam locomotives working between Watford and Amersham.

Before the weekend drivers, firemen and maintenance staff had to travel to London to undergo safety and road learning training, all of which took place at Neasden, the place where steam locomotives used to be based.

The engine we would use was Gresley N2 0-6-2 tank No. 69523, the locomotive having to be fitted with a through air pipe, as the stock was air braked. A brake handle was fitted in the cab and air for the brakes provided by a diesel, or the old Metropolitan electric locomotive *Sara Siddons*. These locomotives were used solely to provide air, but could also be used for propulsion in the event of a steam failure.

Travelling to London on the Friday, we prepared the locomotive, which looked superb in a new coat of paint and fresh from overhaul. Everyone involved was looking forward to a good weekend, although we were also feeling slightly nervous about being on the mainline and using the unfamiliar air brake valve.

After preparations, we backed onto our train at Neasden, ready for our empty stock run to Watford. Given the right away, we were off on the old railway lines that once served the Great Central lines. The engine ran like a dream as speed built up and the inspector was so pleased with the smooth ride, that he increased the speed that the N2 could travel.

At Watford, we ran around our train and waited for our first run to Amersham. Away spot on time, we were told not to loose time, or we could delay any timetabled services.

From Watford, it is mainly down hill to Rickmansworth, where we stopped. The platform was a mass of people, who when on board ensured we had a full train for the climb all the way to Amersham.

Leaving Rickmansworth late due to the crowd, the driver was aware that he had to push the engine so as not delay following trains. However, within a short time, it was obvious the engine was not steaming well. The steam pressure continued to fall slowly back and the boiler water was also falling as we pounded up the bank.

Working really hard, I tried to coax the engine round. The pressure continued to fall with both the driver and myself anxiously watching both steam and water disappear.

"Not far now", said the inspector and on hearing this, the driver kept her going. Reluctant to put on the injector due to the low boiler pressure, we anxiously watched the water almost disappear, while peering ahead looking for Amersham.

Finally, coming to a stand in the platform at Amersham with both injectors on, there was no sign of water in the glass and about 70lb of steam pressure - we had only just made it!

Here, we cleaned the filthy fire, took water and made ready for the return trip, which went without any problems, as most of it was downhill.

It was soon time for our second trip. Leaving Rickmansworth, this time with as much water as possible in the boiler and the steam pressure right on the red line.

However, by the time we reached Amersham the result was the same!

The trips were the same for all the crews, the engine just would not steam while being worked heavy.

For the second day's work, we resorted to an old Midland trick with shy steaming engines, fitting a device called a 'Jimmy' into the blast pipe, a practice which would have you into a lot trouble in B.R. days.

On her first trip, the engine performed better, so a second Jimmy was fitted. This further improved steaming, so that we arrived at Amersham with water in the boiler as we were able to use the injector while climbing the bank.

As all the firemen said afterwards, "That was bloody hard work".

It was even harder cleaning out the mass of dull, lifeless fire that was in the firebox, ready for the next run and this had to be repeated time again and time again. There was no chance of a rest at Amersham between trips with this amount of fire cleaning to be done and it was a good job that the firemen had some help with this task.

All sorts of advice were offered by various people about what sort of shape and type of fire would make this type of engine steam. I tried them all to no avail and finally resorted to what I was used to on the LMS, a wedge-shaped fire, that had been built up well in advance of the heavy climb to Amersham and this worked better than all the other types of fire.

It would have been nice to have a white hot fire, instead of a dull lifeless one!

Before the weekend, I had been promised the chance to drive on one trip by my driver, but after seeing how the engine steamed, the driver obviously did not fancy a go on the shovel, so he never offered me a drive and he had been an ex B.R. fireman.

We had to use the coal supplied by London Underground and this was one of the reasons for the poor steaming.

The combination of the Metropolitan line and the N2 sorted out the men from the boys. Really hard work, but a brilliant weekend, as all the steam weekends were, organised by the men and women of London Underground, who gave their time and effort for free and made donations to charity.

As I mentioned above, during our weekend, we fitted the N2 blast pipe with a 'Jimmy', a device banned during my time on the railways, but despite this, were still used by some footplate crews to improve the blast from the blast pipe and so improve the steaming on engines that were poor steamers. In fact, by the Sunday, two 'Jimmys' had been fitted and steaming had improved slightly, even with this rubbish coal.

Many BR firemen would pay the shed blacksmith, or boilersmith to make them a 'Jimmy', although they would always be removed before going back onto the engine shed, so they would not be caught and disciplined.

Well done everyone at London Underground for giving steam in preservation and volunteer crews the chance to operate on the main line (I will return to the Met. later on).

It was then back to the Great Central Railway, not quite as exciting, but with double track possible in the future, who knows what may happen there.

Large passenger engines were the interest at Loughborough, as at this time we had quite a line up of motive power:

Merchant Navy Class	No. 35005 *Canadian Pacific*
West Country Class	No. 34039 *Boscastle*
West Country Class	No. 34101 *Hartland* (almost ready for steaming)
Jubilee Class	No. 45593 *Kolhapur*
Castle Class	No. 7029 *Clun Castle*
Black 5	No. 45231
Gresley N2	No. 695

The rebuild of Thompson B1 No. 61264 was continuing in the shed.

This must have been the largest number of locomotives seen at any time on the Great Central Railway, although 'guest' engines also visiting at this period included:

Gresley A3	No. 60103 *Flying Scotsman*
Thompson A2	No. 60532 *Blue Peter*
Gresley A4	No. 60007 *Sir Nigel Gresley*
Stanier Coronation Class	No. 46229 *Duchess of Hamilton*

I remember one Sunday, not a Gala, just a normal running day, when the three engines rostered were: *Canadian Pacific, Sir Nigel Gresley* and *Duchess of Hamilton.* What a fabulous line up!

I was privileged to fire and drive all of these famous locomotives, not on the same day, but images of which will live with me forever as the golden era of preservation at the G.C.R. at Loughborough.

Canadian Pacific then began a tour of other preserved railways and I was able to go with her to the East Lancashire Railway and Mid Hants Railway, where we acted as owner's representatives, helping the heritage railway crews get to know the locomotive and getting the chance to drive and fire on another railway.

Later on, *Canadian Pacific* would undergo a complete rebuild and then become one of the main line's star performers, before a burst small tube brought her main line career to a premature halt.

Chapter Eight

Main Line Support Crews

Over the years, I have been asked many times how does someone become a member of a support crew? Also, why are 'support crews' required?

Firstly, you have to have knowledge of how a steam locomotive works, how to maintain it and how to operate it.

With that, you must pass a Personnel Track Safety examination, set by an approved training company approved by Network Rail (as it is at the time of writing). This can only take place after passing a medical, which includes eyesight and hearing tests and all come at a fairly high financial cost to oneself.

These also have to be retaken on a regular basis.

Of course, in addition, you have to know someone who runs a main line approved steam locomotive and who wants support crew.

So, now do I get to ride on the footplate on the main line?

Well, weeks of planning and constant changes take place before running a main line steam trip.

The engine has to be approved for the route, with a path between regular trains being found and approved. This can take weeks, or months, with many changes being made right up to the time the train is due to depart.

Steam approved crews from one of the train operating companies (TOCs) have to be found, as well as a steam approved inspector to oversee the trip.

Coaling, watering and servicing of the locomotive have to be checked and organised in advance. But, most important is the positioning of the locomotive and support coach.

This work is undertaken by either the owner, or members of the support crew. No glamour here then!

The engine and support coach must then be ready to pass a fitness to run examination, before any movement on the main line.

This means some of the support crew could be working two days previous to the trip, much of the time in the open air and without the use of a pit to gain access to the underneath of the engine where so much preparation work takes place. Coaling of the locomotive sometimes has to be done by hand and it's not easy to load 7-tons of coal by hand.

Overhead high voltage cables are a problem on many main lines, especially when trying to service a steam engine.

The day of the trip finally arrives. The engine has steam and been examined and is all ready to go. Some of the crew have already been working long hours in the preparation. We await the arrival of the engine crew and inspector before moving to our start point, which can be some way away.

The engine very often has to be moved hours before departure time of the train, so coal and water have to be preserved where possible.

Finally, we are attached to the train awaiting departure. Coal is pulled forward in the tender, water topped up, if possible and last minute oiling carried out.

Green flag waved, whistle blown and we are away. The support crew is back in the coach, with the exception of one person who rides on the footplate as the owner's representative.

His job is to watch the crew operate the engine correctly and point out anything the crew are not aware of. In addition, he or she must be able to operate the injectors, or brakes in the event of an emergency.

After a time, you become familiar with the crews when you do this regularly and so become part of the team.

I have fired the locomotive many times when it has been my turn to ride on the footplate, so giving the fireman a well-earned break.

After various water stops and finally arriving at the destination, the support crew go into action to service the locomotive, cleaning the fire, emptying the ash from both the smokebox and the ash pan underneath.

All this ash has to be cleared from under the engine and safely disposed of.

Fill the tender both with coal and water, oil all the motion and we are ready for the return journey.

Doing the same on the return as on the outward journey, we finally come to a halt.

Photographs taken and a last look at the engine and all the passengers go home.

Not the support crew! The stock has to be stabled, then the locomotive, which may again be stabled some miles away. Here the engine has to be put to bed. Fire cleaned, boiler filled, then all depends when it is required again, possibly the next day, when support crews are needed again.

It can be five days away from home, just for one main line trip, eating and sleeping in the support coach.

Still want to be in a support crew?

Oh yes! I forgot to mention that no alcohol could be taken during this time, as well as not being paid!

Living and working in very primitive conditions, very often in the cold and wet, but one thing is guaranteed, you will always end up filthy and very tired.

My wife says I must be mad, but she says to see the smile on my face when everything has come together is well worth it, even though it takes a week to get over it nowadays as age creeps up on me.

That is a brief rundown on the support crews, as I have many times been asked why and what do support crews do.

When everything has gone well, there is no better feeling.

But, not everything goes to plan, as anyone who regularly travels on steam trips will know.

Many things contribute to cause delays to these steam trains. The worst thing that can happen for the support crews is some sort of failure of the locomotive, when the crew feel as depressed and disappointed as the passengers.

On my very first trip, I was asked to help Bert Hitchen prepare and run his West

Country Class No. 34027 *Taw Valley*.

The engine was at Toton, my old depot and very close to where I lived at that time. So, the day before the special was due to run, I was involved cleaning and preparing the engine for its journey the next day to Nottingham to Great Yarmouth and return, organised by a company called 'Days Out'.

The start time when the engine left Toton for Nottingham was brought forward, as the engine was still raising steam for the later start time given to us the night before.

Due to all the earlier preparation work, this was not a problem, except that there was no time for breakfast for the support crew.

The start from Nottingham was fine and I was the 'owner's rep' on the footplate. So far, so good.

Reaching Loughborough, we lost time as we were held to allow a late running train ahead of us.

Then, at Melton Mowbray and Oakham, we were delayed further as the train, that was too long to fit into the platforms, was held up as disabled passengers had to be boarded via the double doors in the guard's coach, not in the platform when we first stopped.

The train became later and later as all our paths disappeared.

At the Ely water stop, it was obvious that we didn't have sufficient coal left for the whole journey, even though some spare coal was carried in the support coach. In the event, a diesel had to be hired to take the train on to Norwich, so saving coal, *Taw Valley* then taking over to Great Yarmouth.

All of this had caused a long delay, so our arrival at Great Yarmouth was very late.

Servicing the engine also took a lot longer than allowed for, mainly due to the very low output of the fire hydrant used to fill up the tender with water.

Our departure time had already gone and the engine still had to run to Norwich and back to turn the engine. After much deliberation and complaints from passengers, the decision was taken to run the train with the engine tender first as far as Norwich.

Leaving Norwich with the engine right way, we made our late way back to Nottingham, then while travelling at about 70 mph, the brakes came fully on in the middle of a section.

The reason was a coach generator belt had broken; this in turn hit the vacuum pipe joint, breaking the seal and so applying the brake.

Soon repaired by the support crew, *Taw Valley* set off once more. The problems continued when a fault with the pump that was used to transfer water from a road tanker to our tender failed, so adding more time to our delay.

A wheelchair passenger caused the next delay, not their fault I may add, as the train was too long to fit the platform at Oakham, so the passenger could not alight until the train was moved to allow the disabled coach onto the platform, exactly the same as the outward journey.

Arrival back at Nottingham, if I remember, was about five hours late, the engine and stock then going forwards to Derby for stabling overnight.

Thompson B1 Class No. 61264

I belong to the Thompson B1 Locomotive Trust's B1 No. 61264 support crew, helping out as often as I can, during which I have been involved twice more with failures which have spoilt the day.

One was a hot driving axle box, which resulted in the melting of the white metal bearing. Fortunately, we were able to reach our stop at Norwich and no delays were caused to other trains, but our passengers were obviously disappointed that the engine was not available for the return trip to London. The bonus was that the train was taken on by a new Class 67 diesel, that luckily was available with a driver from Norwich Crown Point.

On another occasion, we had to throw out the fire while on the main line when a small tube joint on the tube plate leaked. This caused a drop in steam pressure and so we were unable to operate the injectors. So, the fire had to be dropped to prevent damage to the boiler.

The first of our problems for this run occurred when the engine had arrived at the EWS depot at Doncaster the day before our trip. A burst water main near to the depot resulted in no water being available at the depot. So, a road tanker had to be quickly organised before we could even start.

From Doncaster, things were OK until we arrived with our train at Scarborough. Here, we were to turn the engine on the turntable, clean the fire and top up the tender with water. Due to the time taken to shunt the train, the time to service the locomotive was drastically reduced, so the support crew had to work even harder.

A late departure, then we were on our way, before being brought to a standstill by signals at the start of the 1:106 Hunmanby bank. With eleven coaches including a generator van behind, No. 61264 had to start a train of 450 tons up this bank. After a few small slips, the locomotive got hold of the train and accelerated up the bank. It was a few miles further on at Hutton Cranswick when things then went wrong. No. 61264 had developed a leaking small tube, with the result that the engine would not steam and the water level could not be maintained in the boiler.

Steam pressure continued to fall, so the train was brought to a stand. Despite trying to raise steam and fill the boiler, without success, the decision was taken to drop the fire to prevent damage to the firebox.

The only good thing was that we were at the side of a small pond, so the red-hot fire, which dropped onto the wooden sleepers, could be extinguished by using water from the pond.

EWS, who were the TOC, then failed to provide an engine, or crew to rescue us. Finally, they hired a diesel locomotive from another company to take our disabled train on.

More bad luck, the engine driver on the diesel did not sign from Hull to Hutton Cranswick. Only the driver of our steam engine signed for the route, but EWS had no way of getting him to the Freightliner locomotive. Unable to hire a taxi, they bribed a photographer to take our driver to Hull to collect the rescue locomotive. It took five hours before we would get underway back to Doncaster and the train arrived back in London many hours later than planned.

The next day, our engine No. 61264 was examined by EWS and found to only have one small tube leaking, but we were told that as a safety precaution, 30 tubes would have to be changed.

With only a week before our next scheduled main line trip, things looked bleak as to the availability of the locomotive.

Members of the Thompson B1 Locomotive Trust quickly sourced some new tubes, collected them and then delivered them to Doncaster.

John Haddow, the boilersmith from the West Coast Railway Company had been quickly called in at very short notice, travelling from Carnforth to Doncaster and thanks must go to the West Coast Railway Company for their co-operation at such short notice on this occasion.

After a superhuman effort during the following week, the engine had 30 flues changed and was steam tested and ready for main line work the following week. Congratulations to all concerned.

The engine then completed a very successful main line trip exactly a week after this failure, running from Cleethorpes to King's Cross as B1 No. 61001 *Eland*.

While riding and firing a Pacific is good, the ride on a two-cylinder B1 at 75mph with eleven coaches on down the East Coast Main Line to King's Cross is something that really tests your skills to the maximum and sets your adrenaline levels to high. It also puts a great big smile on your face!

It a very grey morning at Cleethorpes as we left with a very tight schedule to Doncaster, picking up at stations on the way.

Taking water at Doncaster, the engine had to be pushed on a very tight schedule all the way to Peterborough, where we took water and changed the engine crew. The non-stop run through Grantham was just one of the highlights of this trip, before the assault on the Stoke bank where we passed the summit at nearly 60 mph, before the easier run into Peterborough.

I had the pleasure of being on the footplate for part of this run and also firing while the fireman had a well-earned rest. Coal was well down by Peterborough, mainly due to the tight schedule and heavy acceleration from the stops in the loops to allow GNER trains to overtake us. The worry was would the coal last to London?

Leaving Peterborough, the driver soon had the engine running at the maximum 75-mph allowed and keeping time all the way to London. No loops on this section, so the engine was more economical with the coal and only a signal stop outside King's Cross stopped us arriving on time. The coal left in the tender was low, but we had enough to keep the fire alight until we were able to stable the locomotive.

Part of this run was published in *Steam Railway* magazine by Mike Notley, who described it as a performance to rival the timings of a pacific locomotive.

It is afterwards that you look back and think of all the good performances by both engine and crew, including the support crew and all the other elements coming together to make a success of the whole package. That is the preparation, the actual trip and then the disposal of stock and finally the engine. Then you feel really good!

However, even after a successful trip, things do not always go to plan.

After disposing of the stock, the plan had been to take the engine to a depot for disposal and leave it there, after which the support crew could then make their way home.

We had actually arrived at King's Cross just a few minutes late, due to adverse signals outside the station, which was just after 13.00 hrs, the engine and support coach then moving from King's Cross to Old Oak Common to be stabled.

But, just before our departure, we were informed that Old Oak Common was closed on Saturday afternoons, so we would have to go to Willesden, not far away.

However, as we all knew, Willesden is a depot for electric locomotives and no good at all for a steam engine. Anyway, we had no choice, but to just fill up the boiler and leave the locomotive, which by this time had almost run out of coal.

The support crew then had the task of getting home. After arriving in London at 13.00 hrs, we did not arrive at Willesden until 18.00 hrs. I finally reached home at 00.43 hrs the following morning, almost 12-hours after the train arrived in London and 22-hours after starting the day.

Sometimes you wonder why you do it? Then, you see the photographs (if you're lucky!), read about how well the actual steam trip went and you know why you do it. Brilliant!

The only trouble is that most of the support crews are getting older, then where do we go?

Before a steam train runs on the main line, a supply of water and coal have to be carefully worked out beforehand, however, when unscheduled delays happen, all those careful plans can and do go wrong.

Engines have a limited amount of capacity of coal and water and some itineraries leave little in reserve. Then, if unscheduled stops have to be made for either coal or water, mostly water, then paths are lost and the knock-on effect rapidly causes the late running associated with some steam trips.

While mentioning Thompson B1 No. 61264 and London reminds me of the occasion when this locomotive had first been passed to run on the main line.

At the time painted in lined Apple Green, No. 61264 had been requested to take part in a 'Steam on the Met' weekend of special trains.

I had become a steam engine driver by now and was one of the lucky ones chosen to drive over this particular weekend, the locomotive also running a special train on the Friday before the main event. On this Friday, the driver reported leaks inside the firebox, not too serious and not enough to stop the engine.

I was the driver for the Saturday and after rising early in the morning, we started to prepare the engine for the day's work and by coincidence, my fireman was a boilersmith from the North Yorkshire Railway.

Leaving the sidings at Neasden, we made our way with the stock onto the main line to Harrow-on-the-Hill where signals brought us to a stop. The inspector informed me that the underground train in the adjoining platform would leave simultaneously, so the passengers could take photographs alongside as we ran at speed towards Rickmansworth.

Unfortunately, someone had failed to advise both the signalman and the driver of the underground train. As his signal changed to green, he was away, while ours remained at red. A quick telephone call and we had a green, a touch on the whistle and we were away.

"Can you try to catch him?", said the inspector.

No further instructions as we set off in hot pursuit, not only catching him, but overtaking the underground train, before easing to let him catch up. Then, with adverse signals against the underground train, we went on to Rickmansworth.

The day went fine, although a really hot May Day took its toll on the firemen. They had to work very hard to keep the steam pressure up as we worked really hard up the gradient to Amersham, with trains filled to capacity and a diesel, or electric locomotive at the back to provide the air for the brakes only, although not providing any assistance in running.

Of course, the very hot day and fast scheduled running made the footplate an uncomfortable place to be what with all the dust and heat.

The locomotive also suffered from leaks in the firebox, which resulted in the failure of the engine at the end of the day, despite the valiant efforts of my fireman/boilersmith to caulk the leaks inside a very hot firebox.

The engine ran the second weekend, but only with help from Dennis Howell's pannier tank, coupled up to No. 61264.

The engine had been right on top of the job and looked and sounded magnificent and it just unfortunate that those leaks spoilt the Sunday's running and also the following weekend's running.

One bonus for me during the afternoon running was that the Inspector was Dick Hardy, the former shed master at Stratford, who had fired B1s many times in his younger days.

I had met Dick a few years before when he had fired *Clun Castle* for me on the Great Central Railway in his best suit, while his wife rode in the train. When he realised I was the driver, he changed his turn and asked if he could fire for one round trip? Needless to say, I told him it would be a pleasure.

Leaving Watford, Dick built up his fire ready for the heavy climb from Rickmansworth to Amersham.

Unfortunately, he caught his knuckles on the air brake handle, which was temporarily fitted on the footplate to the right of the driver and which was right in the way of his swing with the shovel. He declined any attention until he had completed his trip at Amersham, but then complained that I had eased the regulator to give him an easier trip.

It was a very hot day and he was 73 years young, but I really wanted him to make the trip. Younger firemen during the day were taking large gulps of fresh air and having a rub down with a damp cloth at the end of each trip and they were not even half his age.

Dick even wrote me a lovely letter afterwards. What a gentleman! What a railwayman!

Some of my early trips out as a member of a support crew were with Merchant Navy Class No. 35005 *Canadian Pacific*. I well remember this, as I did not get to ride on the footplate on my first day, although later I had many trips and many footplate rides on this locomotive, including taking my turn with the shovel.

Two trips will be specially remembered. The first was from Alton in Hampshire, to Tyseley in Birmingham, engine and support coach only.

The driver allowed me to drive as far as Oxford, which was very unusual and then I fired to Tyseley.

The second one was on my fifty-six birthday, which was 40 years to the day that I had been first been on the footplate. No. 35005 *Canadian Pacific* was working from Birmingham International to York and return.

As I had fired to York as a young man, I was to fire to York again this day. On the return trip a special surprise cake, complete with candles was presented to me in the support coach. In the old days of steam, I am sure we would have had a drink to go with it, but nowadays this is strictly taboo, so the choice was tea or coffee.

The owner of *Canadian Pacific* then was Andrew Naish. Thanks Andrew for some great times and especially for my birthday treat.

When Andrew sold *Canadian Pacific* to be based in the south, I decided then that it was too far away for me to be on the support crew.

Other trips I did were with Bert Hitchens's, *Taw Valley* on some of the ill-fated 'Days Out' Trips.

One aspect I have not mentioned since becoming part of a support crew, is the regular summer working in Scotland of 'The Jacobite'. For the people who do not know, this service operates a regular steam hauled service throughout the summer, operated by the West Coast Railway Company from Fort William to Mallaig and return daily. This is most certainly one of the great train journeys in the world.

Running from late May through to late September each year, two steam engines are used through the season, being based at Fort William. Here, the engines are prepared and then serviced after each trip.

The support crews usually stay in their support coach, again stabled at Fort William. Most commit a week at a time to have a hard working week's holiday doing what they enjoy most. Due to the length of time in Scotland, the regular support crews for these engines do not have sufficient manpower to cover this period. So, other groups of qualified support crews come together during the weeks to help to maintain this service.

Our engine, No. 61264, in 2006 ran this service for the sixth consecutive year.

2006 also saw three engines working the service during the season, proving how popular and successful this service is.

The season starts with the run to Scotland, starting from the West Coast Railway Company base at Carnforth, the first two engines double-heading the train to Fort William. This trip alone is superb, but does not carry passengers. Then after a long Summer season and into Autumn it is time to return to Carnforth with the engines and coaches.

Then, it is home for the weary crews, before starting work on all the necessary maintenance on the locomotives after a hard working summer and getting them ready for any more work, either on the main line, or one of the preserved railways around the country.

At the end of the 2005 season No.61264 worked a special train from Fort William to Glasgow Queen's Street station. This was the return working of a special train that had earlier started in Glasgow, working to Fort William and Mallaig, using two other steam engines.

Leaving Fort William late, we set off for Glasgow with a crew from West Coast Railways. Due to earlier problems at Fort William our fireman was unable to work the train, so a young man who worked at the National Railway Museum at York, who initially had asked to ride in our support coach, was asked to fire the engine from Fort William to Carnforth. He had only recently passed out as a fireman for West Coast Railways and had not fired on such a journey.

What a test he was facing! After a severe test climbing virtually all the way to Corrour, almost 27 miles before the climb from Rannock to Gortan and then the six-mile climb from Bridge of Orchy to Tyndrum before the descent into Crianlarich, where we took water. The engine crew then having a well-earned breather, while watering and servicing of the locomotive took place. During this time, smart work by the support crew gained some time back as we set off for Glasgow and the steep climb to Glen Douglas.

A really excellent performance by both the crew and the engine, enabled the time to be regained to our Glasgow arrival, just a few minutes late, the first steam arrival since the end of steam in the 1960s.

After many photographs, the engine finally departed for St Rollox Works for overnight stabling, probably St Rollox being where some of the parts of No. 61264 were originally manufactured in 1947.

The following day, No. 61264 left with the empty stock for Carnforth via Eastfield shed, where B1 engines were stationed in the steam era, No. 61264 carrying a 65A Eastfield shed plate.

A very fast run up the West Coast Main Line over Beattock and through Carlisle, up and over Shap mostly at the 75-mph limit, before the downhill section to Carnforth, making a two-hour early arrival at Carnforth, mainly due to missing out on the various loop stops that had been scheduled for us.

This had been a very hard inaugural run for our very young fireman, but what an excellent job he had done. I know that after the first day's run from Fort William to Glasgow, he had gone to bed a very tired, but proud fireman.

Nonetheless, after arriving at the engine the next day feeling very stiff, he had to request some assistance with the shovel for the run to Carnforth!

Disposing the engine at Carnforth, some of the support crew went home, while the remainder stayed at Carnforth to prepare the engine for its next trip, which was to the Crewe Engine Works Open Day, less than a week away.

This would be followed by a move to our new home at Barrow Hill, then only a few days later a move to the North Yorkshire Moors Railway.

I have no idea how long I will be able to carry on doing what I do. This will, of course, depend on my physical condition and if I can still pass the necessary medical examinations required.

I still drive at the Great Central Railway at Loughborough, as and when required and hope to continue as long as possible.

Also, when free time allows, I like to go the shed at Loughborough to do my little bit helping in the maintenance and cleaning, or whatever needs doing and there is always something to do. Steam engines just generate more and more work, all dirty and mostly physical.

The sight and sound of a steam locomotive hard at work at the head of a train is the reward for all the hard work of not just the crew, but all the many people who have done their bit to ensure the steam engine will never die.

Thanks to you all.

FOOTNOTE: As I was completing this manuscript, disaster struck at Fort William when No. 61264 suffered a smashed cylinder casting when preparing for the day's service to Mallaig - the result of water in the cylinders.

The locomotive was then taken to Carnforth for lengthy and costly repairs to be carried out. The cylinder casting was removed and sent to a specialist cast iron welders at Coalville for repairs. Although an expensive job, it should then be stronger than the original.

Since then the locomotive and support coach have been moved by road back to our base at Barrow Hill. Here the cylinder casting will be refitted and relined, then new pistons fitted and all the motion reassembled.

This work is expected to be completed by early 2007.